Juvenile Suicide in Confinement: A National Survey

OJJDP Report

Lindsay M. Hayes
National Center on Institutions and Alternatives

February 2009

NCJ 213691

Acknowledgments

Staff collaboration is a critical ingredient in an effective suicide prevention program. The task of completing the first national survey of juvenile suicide in confinement could not have been accomplished without the collaborative efforts of a project team comprising prominent juvenile justice practitioners and researchers. The team—which included G. David Curry, Ph.D., Department of Criminology, University of Missouri-St. Louis; Robert E. DeComo, Ph.D., Director of Research, National Council on Crime and Delinquency; Barbara C. Dooley, Ph.D., former Director, Madison County (TN) Juvenile Court Services; Cedrick Heraux, Ph.D. candidate, School of Criminal Justice, Michigan State University; and David W. Roush, Ph.D., Director, Center for Research and Professional Development, Michigan State University—was instrumental in the design of the data collection instruments, analysis of the data, and review of the draft report. Alice Boring of the National Center on Institutions and Alternatives brought the report together in its final form.

In addition, the Council of Juvenile Correctional Administrators (CJCA) and the National Juvenile Detention Association (NJDA), provided invaluable assistance in endorsing the project and encouraging juvenile facility directors to participate in the survey, as well as in reviewing the draft. Special thanks is extended to CJCA's Edward J. Loughran, Kim Godfrey, and Robert Dugan and NJDA's Earl L. Dunlap and Michael A. Jones.

The support of officials and staff at the Office of Juvenile Justice and Delinquency Prevention, in particular, Program Managers Karen Stern and Phelan Wyrick, is appreciated.

Table of Contents

Acknowledgments..

List of Tables ....

Executive Summary ....

Introduction..1
    Prevalence 1
    Risk Factors 1
        Mental Disorders and Substance Abuse 1
        Physical, Sexual, and Emotional Abuse 2
        Self-Injurious Behavior..3
    Provision of Mental Health Services in Juvenile Facilities 4
    Surveillance Data on Adult and Juvenile Suicide...4

Data Collection 6
    Phase 1 6
    Phase 2 7

Findings...9
    Personal Characteristics of the Victim...9
        Race...9
        Sex...9
        Age...10
        Living Arrangement Before Confinement 10
        Most Serious Offense..11
        Additional Charges 11
        Confinement Status...11
        Most Serious Prior Offenses 12
        Length of Confinement (Before Suicide) 12
        Substance Abuse 13
        Medical Problems 13
        Emotional Abuse...14
        Physical Abuse..14
        Sexual Abuse 14
        Mental Illness..15
        Prior Suicidal Behavior...15
        History of Room Confinement...15
    Suicide Incident Characteristics...16
        Date...16
        Time...16
        Method, Instrument, and Anchoring Device..17
        Intoxication 18

Room Assignment..18
Time Span..18
Room Confinement..18
Suicide Precaution Status..19
Assessment by Qualified Mental Health Professional..19
Juvenile Facility Characteristics 20
Facility Type and Population 20
Written Suicide Prevention Policy..21
Intake Screening for Suicide Risk..21
Suicide Prevention Training 21
Certification in Cardiopulmonary Resuscitation 22
Suicide Precaution Protocol..22
Safe Housing...23
Mortality Review 23

Special Considerations..25
Comprehensive Suicide Prevention Programming 25
Room Confinement 26
Corrective Action 28

Conclusion 30
Comprehensive Suicide Prevention Programming 30
Staff Training 32
Detention Centers..32
Data Limitations..33
Research 34
Challenges 34

Notes 35

References..38

Appendix A: Phase 1 Survey Instrument...45

Appendix B: Phase 2 Survey Instrument...48

List of Tables

Table 1: Sources Used To Identify the Number of Juvenile Suicides in Confinement, 1995–1995 7

Table 2: Suicides in Juvenile Facilities, 1995–1999, by Victim's Race and Facility Type 9

Table 3: Suicides in Juvenile Facilities, 1995–1999, by Victim's Sex and Facility Type 10

Table 4: Suicides in Juvenile Facilities, 1995–1999, by Victim's Age and Facility Type.......................10

Table 5: Suicides in Juvenile Facilities, 1995–1999, by Victim's Living Arrangement (Before Confinement) and Facility Type 10

Table 6: Suicides in Juvenile Facilities, 1995–1999, by Victim's Most Serious Offense and Facility Type 11

Table 7: Suicides in Juvenile Facilities, 1995–1999, by Victim's Confinement Status and Facility Type 12

Table 8: Suicides in Juvenile Facilities by Victims With Prior Offenses, 1995–1999, by Victim's Most Serious Prior Offense and Facility Type..12

Table 9: Suicides in Juvenile Facilities, 1995–1999, by Victim's Length of Confinement (Before Suicide) and Facility Type 13

Table 10: Suicides in Juvenile Facilities, 1995–1999, by Victim's History of Substance Abuse and Facility Type 13

Table 11: Suicides in Juvenile Facilities, 1995–1999, by Victim's History of Medical Problems and Facility Type 13

Table 12: Suicides in Juvenile Facilities, 1995–1999, by Victim's History of Emotional Abuse and Facility Type 14

Table 13: Suicides in Juvenile Facilities, 1995–1999, by Victim's History of Physical Abuse and Facility Type 14

Table 14: Suicides in Juvenile Facilities, 1995–1999, by Victim's History of Sexual Abuse and Facility Type 14

Table 15: Suicides in Juvenile Facilities, 1995–1999, by Victim's History of Mental Illness and Facility Type 15

Table 16: Suicides in Juvenile Facilities, 1995–1999, by Victim's Prior Suicidal Behavior and Facility Type 15

Table 17: Suicides in Juvenile Facilities, 1995–1999, by Victim's History of Room Confinement and Facility Type 16

Table 18: Suicides in Juvenile Facilities, 1995–1999, by Year of Suicide and Facility Type 16

Table 19: Suicides in Juvenile Facilities, 1995–1999, by Time of Suicide and Facility Type..................17

Table 20: Suicides by Hanging in Juvenile Facilities, 1995–1999, by Instrument Used and Facility Type 17

Table 21: Suicides by Hanging in Juvenile Facilities, 1995–1999, by Anchoring Device Used and Facility Type 17

Table 22: Suicides in Juvenile Facilities, 1995–1999, by Time Span Between Last Observation and Finding Victim and Facility Type..18

Table 23: Suicides in Juvenile Facilities, 1995–1999, by Victim's Room Confinement Status and Facility Type 18

Table 24: Suicides in Juvenile Facilities, 1995–1999, by Victim's Suicide Precaution Status and Facility Type 19

Table 25: Suicides in Juvenile Facilities, 1995–1999, by Victim's Assessment by a Qualified Mental Health Professional (QMHP) and Facility Type..19

Table 26: Suicides in Juvenile Facilities by Victims Who Were Assessed by a Qualified Mental Health Professional (QMHP), 1995–1999, by Time of Victim's Last Contact With QMHP and Facility Type 20

Table 27: Suicides in Juvenile Facilities, 1995–1999, by Population of Facility and Facility Type.........20

Table 28: Suicides in Juvenile Facilities, 1995–1999, by Facility's Maintenance of a Written Suicide Prevention Policy and Facility Type..21

Table 29: Suicides in Juvenile Facilities, 1995–1999, by Intake Screening of Victim for Suicide Risk and Facility Type 21

Table 30: Suicides in Juvenile Facilities, 1995–1999, by Facility's Provision of Suicide Prevention Training and Facility Type...21

Table 31: Suicides in Juvenile Facilities That Provide Suicide Prevention Training, 1995–1999, by Frequency of (Annual) Training and Facility Type...22

Table 32: Suicides in Juvenile Facilities That Provide Suicide Prevention Training, 1995–1999, by Duration of Training and Facility Type 22

Table 33: Suicides in Juvenile Facilities, 1995–1999, by Staff Certification in Cardiopulmonary Resuscitation (CPR) and Facility Type 22

Table 34: Suicides in Juvenile Facilities, 1995–1999, by Facility's Maintenance of a Suicide Precaution Protocol and Facility Type 23

Table 35: Suicides in Juvenile Facilities That Maintain a Suicide Prevention Protocol, 1995–1999, by Highest Frequency Level of Observation and Facility Type 23

Table 36: Suicides in Juvenile Facilities, 1995–1999, by Facility's Provision of Safe Housing for Suicidal Youth and Facility Type 23

Table 37: Suicides in Juvenile Facilities, 1995–1999, by Mortality Review of Suicide and Facility Type 24

Table 38: Suicides in Juvenile Facilities, 1995–1999, by Number of Suicide Prevention Components Implemented by the Facility and Facility Type 26

Executive Summary

Although youth suicide in the community has been identified as a major public health problem, juvenile suicide in confinement has received scant attention. The Office of Juvenile Justice and Delinquency Prevention (OJJDP) awarded a contract to National Center on Institutions and Alternatives to conduct the first national survey on juvenile suicide in confinement. The primary goal was to determine the extent and distribution of juvenile suicides in confinement (i.e., juvenile detention centers, reception centers, training schools, ranches, camps, and farms). The survey gathered descriptive data on the demographic characteristics of each victim, the characteristics of the incident, and the characteristics of the juvenile facility in which the suicide took place.

The study identified 110 juvenile suicides occurring between 1995 and 1999. Data was analyzed on 79 cases. Of these 79 suicides, 41.8 percent occurred in training school/secure facilities, 36.7 percent in detention centers, 15.2 percent in residential treatment centers, and 6.3 percent in reception/diagnostic centers. Almost half (48.1 percent) the suicides occurred in facilities administered by state agencies, 39.2 percent took place in county facilities, and 12.7 percent occurred in private programs. Highlights of the data include:

❖ More than two-thirds (68.4 percent) of victims were Caucasian.

❖ A substantial majority (79.7 percent) of victims were male.

❖ Average (mean) age of victims was 15.7, with more than 70 percent of victims ages 15–17.

❖ A sizable number (38.0 percent) of victims were living with one parent at time of confinement.

❖ More than two-thirds (69.6 percent) of victims were confined for nonviolent offenses.

❖ Approximately two-thirds (67.1 percent) of victims were held on commitment status at time of death, with 32.9 percent on detained status; the vast majority (79.3 percent) of victims held in detention centers were on detained status.

❖ A substantial majority (78.5 percent) of victims had a history of prior offenses; most of these (72.7 percent) were of a nonviolent nature.

❖ With the exception of detention centers, deaths were evenly distributed during a more than 12-month period, with the same number of suicides occurring within the first 3 days of confinement as occurring after more than 10 months of confinement; only 3.8 percent of all suicides occurred within the first 24 hours of confinement.

❖ All detention center suicides occurred within the first 4 months of confinement, with more than 40 percent occurring within the first 72 hours.

❖ Nearly three-quarters (73.4 percent) of victims had a history of substance abuse, 19.0 percent had a history of medical problems, 44.3 percent had a history of emotional abuse, 34.2 percent had a history of physical abuse, and 27.8 percent had a history of sexual abuse.

❖ A majority (65.8 percent) of victims had a history of mental illness (with 65.3 percent of these victims suffering from depression at the time of death); 53.5 percent of victims were taking psychotropic medications.

❖ More than two-thirds (69.6 percent) of victims had a history of suicidal behavior, with suicide attempt(s) the most frequent type of suicidal behavior (45.5 percent), followed by suicidal ideation/threat (30.9 percent) and suicidal gesture/self-mutilation (23.6 percent).

❖ Approximately half (50.6 percent) of suicides occurred during a 6-hour period between 6 p.m. and midnight, and almost a third (29.1 percent) occurred between 6 p.m. and 9 p.m.; 70.9 percent of suicides occurred during traditional waking hours (6 a.m. to 9 p.m.), and 29.1 percent occurred during nonwaking hours (9 p.m. to 6 a.m.).

❖ Almost all (98.7 percent) the suicides were by hanging; 71.8 percent of these victims used their bedding (e.g., sheet, blanket) as the instrument. A variety of anchoring devices were used in the hangings, including door hinge/knob (20.5 percent), air vent (19.2 percent), bedframe (19.2 percent), and window frame (14.1 percent).

❖ None of the victims was under the influence of alcohol or drugs at the time of the suicide.

❖ Almost three-quarters (74.7 percent) of victims were assigned to single-occupancy rooms.

❖ Approximately 41 percent of victims were found in less than 15 minutes after the last observation of the youth: however, slightly more than 15 percent of victims were found more than 1 hour after last being seen alive.

❖ About half (50.6 percent) the victims were on room confinement status at the time of death (and 62.0 percent of victims had a history of room confinement). The circumstances that led to room confinement at the time of death included failure to follow program rules/inappropriate behavior (47.3 percent), threat/actual physical abuse of staff or peers (42.1 percent), and other (10.6 percent). Only 16.7 percent of residential treatment center victims were on room confinement status at time of death.

❖ A large majority (85.0 percent) of victims who died by suicide while on room confinement status died during waking hours (6 a.m. to 9 p.m.), a higher percentage than those victims who died by suicide during waking hours but were not on room confinement status (70.9 percent).

❖ A small percentage (16.5 percent) of victims were on suicide precaution status at time of death, most of whom were required to be observed at 15-minute intervals. Despite their identified risk, almost half of these victims were found to be last observed in excess of the required 15-minute interval.

❖ More than two-thirds (69.6 percent) of victims were assessed by a qualified mental health professional before their death (although only 34.5 percent of detention center victims received such assessments); slightly less than half (44.3 percent) of all victims either had never been assessed by a qualified mental health professional or had not been assessed within 30 days of their death.

❖ Only 37.9 percent of the suicides took place in facilities that provided annual suicide prevention training to its direct care staff.

❖ Although a large majority (78.5 percent) of victims died in facilities that maintained a written suicide prevention policy at time of suicide, only 20.3 percent of victims were in facilities that had all seven suicide prevention components (written policy, intake screening, training, CPR certification, observation, safe housing, and mortality review) at time of suicide. The degree to which suicides took place in facilities that had all seven suicide prevention components varied considerably by facility type: detention centers (10.3 percent), training schools/secure facilities (24.2 percent), reception/diagnostic centers (40.0 percent), and residential treatment centers (25.0 percent).

The study offers several recommendations, including the following:

❖ Consistent with national corrections standards and practices, juvenile facilities, regardless of size and type, should have a detailed written suicide prevention policy that addresses each of the following critical components: training, identification/screening, communication, housing, levels of supervision, intervention, reporting, and followup/mortality review.

❖ Juvenile facility administrators should create and maintain effective training programs and ensure that direct care, medical, and mental health personnel receive both pre-service and annual instruction in suicide prevention. Young lives will continue to be lost and jurisdictions will incur liability from these tragic deaths unless facility personnel receive adequate training.

❖ Suicide prevention training curriculums used in juvenile facilities have historically relied on information gathered about adult inmate suicide and youth suicide in the community. Given the findings from this study, which demonstrate differences between adult inmate suicide and juvenile suicide, development of separate training curriculums targeted to suicide prevention within juvenile facilities appears warranted.

❖ Significant deficiencies in intake screening and a lack of suicide prevention programs in detention centers experiencing suicides warrant immediate attention. Resources need to be channeled to facilities housing juveniles, particularly detention centers, to ensure basic, yet comprehensive, suicide prevention programming, including intake screening for suicide risk.

❖ The fact that more than one-third of the suicides identified in this study were unknown to government agencies responsible for the care and advocacy of confined youth is a cause for concern. Each death within a juvenile facility should be accounted for, comprehensively reviewed, and provisions made for corrective action as warranted.

❖ Research efforts should be directed at determining additional precipitating factors to juvenile suicide, the perceived relationship between suicide and room confinement, and the effect, if any, of prolonged confinement on suicidal behavior.

Findings from this study pose formidable challenges for juvenile correctional and healthcare officials and their staffs. For example, although room confinement remains a standard procedure in most juvenile facilities, its potential consequences need to be weighed carefully. Moreover, because data show that suicides can occur at any time during a youth's confinement, a continuum of comprehensive suicide prevention services aimed at the collaborative identification, continued assessment, and safe management of youth at risk for self-harm is required.

Introduction

This introduction provides a review of the literature on juvenile suicide in confinement. It examines the prevalence of juvenile suicide in the general population, highlights risk factors for juvenile suicide, assesses the provision of mental health services in juvenile facilities, and presents data on adult and juvenile suicide in confinement.

Prevalence

According to the Surgeon General of the United States, youth suicide in the general population is a national tragedy and a major public health problem (Carmona, 2005; U.S. Department of Health and Human Services, 1999). The suicide rate of young people (ages 15 to 24) has tripled from 2.7 per 100,000 in 1950 to 9.9 per 100,000 in 2001 (Arias et al., 2003). More teenagers die from suicide than from cancer, heart disease, AIDS, birth defects, stroke, pneumonia and influenza, and chronic lung disease combined (U.S. Department of Health and Human Services, 1999). In addition, a recent national survey found that more than 3 million youth are at risk for suicide each year in the community, with 37 percent of surveyed youth reporting that they attempted suicide during the previous 12 months (Substance Abuse and Mental Health Services Administration, 2001).

Despite the fact that youth suicide in the general population is considered a major public health problem, as well as the fact that several national studies have been conducted regarding the extent and nature of suicide in jail and prison facilities (Hayes, 1989, 1995), comparable national research has not been conducted regarding juvenile suicide in confinement.[1]

Risk Factors

Brent (1995) has identified mental disorder and substance abuse as the most important set of risk factors for adolescent suicide in the general population. Other risk factors include impulsive aggression, parental depression and substance abuse, family discord and abuse, and poor family support. Life stressors—specifically interpersonal conflict and loss, as well as legal and disciplinary problems—were also associated with suicidal behavior in adolescents, particularly those who were substance abusers. It has been argued that many of these risk factors are prevalent in youth confined in juvenile facilities (Alessi et al., 1984; Rohde, Seeley, and Mace, 1997). Recently, Sanislow et al. (2003) found that high levels of depression and hopelessness and the acute situational stress of incarceration might explain why confined youth had levels of psychological distress similar to those of severely disturbed adolescents hospitalized on an acute psychiatric inpatient unit. Therefore, if all youth are to some degree at risk for suicide, juveniles in confinement may be at greater risk because they have life histories that predispose them to suicide (e.g., mental disorders and substance abuse; physical, sexual, and emotional abuse; and current and prior self-injurious behavior).

Mental Disorders and Substance Abuse

The prevalence of mental disorders among confined youth has been studied in several states. A California study found that 32 percent of confined male juveniles met the criteria for post-traumatic stress disorder and that these youth experienced increased levels of distress, anxiety, and depression while exhibiting lower levels of restraint, impulse control, and suppression of aggression (Steiner, Garcia, and Matthews, 1997). In Mississippi, a study found that at least 66 percent of confined youth met the *Diagnostic and Statistical Manual* (DSM-IV) criteria for a mental disorder, with more than half the youth suffering from multiple disorders including conduct disorder and substance abuse (Robertson and Husain, 2001). In Maryland, some 57 percent of confined youth self-reported a prior mental health history (Shelton, 2000). In Virginia, more than 60 percent of youth admitted to the state's juvenile reception and diagnostic center were identified with a mental health treatment need (McGarvey and Waite, 2000). In Georgia, 61 percent of confined youth were found to have mental health disorders (Marsteller et al., 1997). In comparing rates of mental disorder for juveniles in confinement with rates for youth in the general population, the Georgia researchers found substantially higher rates for juveniles in confinement (61 percent versus 22 percent for any disorder, 30 percent versus 11 percent for anxiety disorders, and 13 percent versus 4 percent for depression). In Texas, researchers found that detention center youth had a high prevalence of psychiatric disorders, usually undiagnosed, and that comorbidity was common (Domalanta et al., 2003). Preliminary data from an ongoing longitudinal analysis of mental disorders among 1,830 youth confined in a county juvenile detention center in Illinois suggest that two-thirds of the youth have one or more alcohol, drug, or mental disorders, thus projecting that more than 670,000 youth processed into the juvenile justice system throughout the country each year would meet the diagnostic criteria for one or more alcohol, drug, or mental disorders (Teplin et al., 2002).

In sum, following two comprehensive reviews of the literature (Otto et al., 1992; Edens and Otto, 1997), youth in confinement have been estimated to experience the following rates of mental disorders:

❖ Conduct disorders (50–90 percent).
❖ Attention deficit disorders (up to 46 percent).
❖ Anxiety disorders (6–41 percent).
❖ Substance abuse or dependence (25–50 percent).
❖ Affective disorders (32–78 percent).
❖ Psychotic disorder (1–6 percent).
❖ Co-occurring mental health and substance abuse disorders (more than 50 percent).

Thus, significant rates of mental disorders, particularly conduct disorder, have been consistently reported for youth in confinement. Because DSM-IV criteria for conduct disorder include "aggressive conduct that causes or threatens physical harm to other people or animals, non-aggressive conduct that causes property loss or damage, deceitfulness or theft, and serious violations of rule" (American Psychiatric Association, 2000:94), the high rates of this disorder among incarcerated youth are not surprising. In conclusion, two facts appear undisputed—a high percentage of youth in the juvenile justice system have a diagnosable mental disorder, and these juveniles have higher rates of mental disorders than youth in the general population (Cocozza and Skowyra, 2000).

Physical, Sexual, and Emotional Abuse

Juveniles in confinement also have higher rates of physical, sexual, and emotional abuse than adolescents in the community. Shelton (2000) found that confined youth in Maryland had high rates of self-reported physical (35 percent) and sexual (18 percent) abuse; however, Chapman and colleagues (2000) found that detained juveniles in Connecticut had lower rates of physical abuse (11 percent) and sexual abuse (10 percent). Esposito and Clum (2002) found higher rates of self-reported physical (58 percent) and sexual (24 percent) abuse for confined youth. With regard to suicide, confined youth who reported a history of sexual abuse had a 43-percent incidence of suicidal ideation and a 35-percent incidence of one or more suicide attempts, whereas youth who reported no history of sexual abuse had an 18-percent suicidal ideation rate and a 12-percent rate of suicide attempts (Morris et al., 1995).

Self-Injurious Behavior

Although little research has been conducted regarding youth suicide in custody, the information that is available suggests a high prevalence of self-injurious behavior in juvenile correctional facilities. For example, according to one national study, more than 11,000 juveniles are estimated to engage in more than 17,000 incidents of suicidal behavior in juvenile facilities each year (Parent et al., 1994). In 1991, a modified version of the Centers for Disease Control's Youth Risk Behavior Surveillance System survey was administered to more than 1,800 confined youth in 39 juvenile institutions across the United States (Morris et al., 1995). The study found that almost 22 percent of confined youth seriously considered suicide, 20 percent made a plan, 16 percent made at least one attempt, and 8 percent were injured in a suicide attempt during the previous 12 months.

Other studies found that significant percentages of detained youth had histories of suicide attempts (Dembo et al., 1990) and current suicidal behavior (Robertson and Husain, 2001, Shelton, 2000; Davis et al., 1991; Woolf and Funk, 1985). In fact, Robertson and Husain (2001) found that 31 percent of confined youth self-reported a suicide attempt, and 9 percent were currently suicidal with either ideation and/or a plan to act on suicidal thoughts. Finally, Chowanec et al. (1991) found higher rates of self-harm behavior among incarcerated male youth than in the general adolescent community population.

Caucasian youth appear to attempt suicide in confinement at a higher rate than African American youth (Kempton and Forehand, 1992; Alessi et al., 1984). Morris and colleagues (1995) found that Native American and Caucasian youth reported higher rates of suicidal ideation (29 percent and 25 percent, respectively) than Hispanic, Asian, and African American youth (15 percent, 12 percent, and 8 percent, respectively). Other researchers have reported similar findings of high rates of suicidal behavior among Native American youth confined in juvenile facilities (Duclos, LeBeau, and Elias, 1994).[2]

Several studies consistently found that certain risk factors point to increased rates of suicidal behavior for incarcerated youth. For example, researchers have reported that confined youth with either major affective disorder or borderline personality disorder have a higher degree of suicidal ideation and more suicide attempts than adolescents in the general population (Alessi et al., 1984); incarcerated male youth whose parents had affectionless bonding styles also reported more suicidal ideation and/or attempts (McGarvey et al., 1999). Findings from another study indicate that more than half (52 percent) of all detained youth self-reported current suicidal ideation, with 33 percent having a history of suicidal behavior (Esposito and Clum, 2002). The researchers concluded that a history of sexual abuse "directly affects the development of suicidal ideation and behavior in incarcerated adolescents" (Esposito and Clum, 2002:145).

In addition, a study of youth confined in a juvenile detention facility found that suicidal behavior in males was most significantly associated with depression, major life events (such as court involvement, death of a family member, etc.), poor social connections, and past suicide attempts, whereas suicidal behavior in females was associated with impulsivity, current depression, instability, and younger age (Mace, Rohde, and Gnau, 1997; Rohde, Seeley, and Mace, 1997). The most common correlate between males and females was not living with a biological parent before detention. Suicidal behavior of a friend was significantly associated with past and current suicidal ideation among boys, but not girls (Rohde, Seeley, and Mace, 1997).

Finally, a study of confined youth referred for psychiatric assessment found that 30 percent reported suicidal ideation/behavior and 30 percent reported self-mutilative behavior while incarcerated (Penn et al., 2003). These youth reported more depression, anxiety, and anger than nonsuicidal confined youth.

Provision of Mental Health Services in Juvenile Facilities

The mental health status of confined youth and the general conditions of confinement within juvenile correctional systems have increasingly come under scrutiny. Attention has been limited generally to investigations of specific jurisdictions or anecdotal information on tragic outcomes (Amnesty International, 1998; Burrell, 1999; Coalition for Juvenile Justice, 1999, 2000; Puritz and Scali, 1998; Rosenbaum, 1999; Sullivan, 1995; Trupin and Patterson, 2003; Twedt, 2001a, 2001b; U.S. House of Representatives, 2004).

In 1994, the Office of Juvenile Justice and Delinquency Prevention (OJJDP) released a landmark study, *Conditions of Confinement: Juvenile Detention and Corrections Facilities,* about the conditions of confinement in juvenile facilities (Parent et al., 1994). It included a survey of 984 public and private detention centers, reception and diagnostic centers, training schools, and ranches throughout the country. On a daily basis, these facilities held almost 65,000 juveniles or 69 percent of youth confined in the United States. Substantial and widespread problems in living space, health care, security, and the control of suicidal behavior were found in the surveyed facilities.

With regard to the state of mental health services for confined youth throughout the country, a 1983 national survey of healthcare delivery in juvenile correctional facilities found deficiencies in certain key areas: only 60 percent of facilities were conducting initial health screening and less than 50 percent were providing ongoing mental health services (Anno, 1984). Fifteen years later, in 1998, a national survey found increased availability of mental health services in juvenile facilities, but that gaps still remained: 64 percent of facilities provided initial mental health screening, 74 percent provided a clinical evaluation by mental health staff, 82 percent had provisions for psychotropic medication, and 69 percent provided onsite access to psychiatrists, psychologists, and/or master's degree level social workers (Goldstrom et al., 2001).

Surveillance Data on Adult and Juvenile Suicide

Suicide is a leading cause of death within jails throughout the country. Suicide ranks third (behind natural causes and AIDS) as the leading cause of death in prisons (Bureau of Justice Statistics, 2005). Close to 200 inmates commit suicide in state and federal prisons each year, and the rate of suicide in prisons, though far below that for jail suicides, is greater than that for the general population (Hayes, 1995). Most research on prison suicide has found that the vast majority of victims are convicted of personal crimes, housed in single cells, and have a history of suicide attempts and/or mental illness (Bonner, 1992; He et al., 2001; White and Schimmel, 1995).

Although several national studies have been conducted about the extent and nature of suicide in jail and prison facilities, comparable national research has not been conducted about juvenile suicide in confinement. The 1988 Amendments to the Juvenile Justice and Delinquency Prevention Act of 1974 established an annual requirement for OJJDP to provide a detailed summary and analysis of the most recent juvenile custody data on the number and individual characteristics of juveniles taken into custody, rates at which they are taken into custody, number of juveniles who died in custody, and circumstances of their deaths. In response to this mandate, OJJDP established the Research Program on Juveniles Taken into Custody in 1989. The survey program included data collected from the State Juvenile Corrections System Reporting Program and the Children in Custody (CIC) Census. In 1988, the first year of the CIC survey, state officials reported 17 suicides occurring in public detention centers, reception/diagnostic centers, and training schools throughout the country (Krisberg et al., 1991). In 1993, 14 such suicides were reported (Austin et al., 1995). Other than listing the gender of the victim, facility type, and region of the country, the OJJDP census was unable to collect data on the circumstances surrounding these suicides. As stated by the authors as a preface to one of the survey reports:

> ...information available on characteristics of juveniles admitted is inadequate. While most facilities record specific demographic, legal, and other information for administrative or operational purposes, no mechanism exists to collect and synthesize these data on a national level for research, policy, or program development purposes. (DeComo et al., 1995:1)

In 1997, OJJDP inaugurated a successor to the CIC Census series that included both a Census of Juveniles in Residential Placement (CJRP) and a Juvenile Residential Facility Census (JRFC). The goal of JRFC is to collect information on facility environments and services, including facility ownership, security features, bed space and crowding, staffing, physical and mental health care, education and substance abuse programming, and deaths in custody. According to the 2000 JRFC, 10 juvenile suicides were reported during the most recent 12-month reporting period (OJJDP, 2002).[3] Similar to the CIC series, the JRFC is unable to collect data on the circumstances surrounding these suicides.

The current CJRP and JRFC research programs remain the only source of nationwide data regarding juveniles in custody. Given the limitations described above, no data source is currently available to adequately document the extent and nature of juvenile suicide in confinement.[4]

Data Collection

In August 1999, the Office of Juvenile Justice and Delinquency Prevention (OJJDP) awarded a contract to the National Center on Institutions and Alternatives to conduct the first national survey on juvenile suicide in confinement.[5] The primary goal was to determine the extent and distribution of juvenile suicides in confinement and to gather descriptive data on the characteristics of each victim, incident, and juvenile facility in which the suicide occurred. A report of the survey's findings would serve as a resource for juvenile justice practitioners to expand their knowledge and for juvenile correctional administrators to create and/or revise policies and training curriculums on suicide prevention. Data collection occurred in two phases.

Phase 1

During the initial phase, a 1-page survey instrument and cover letter was sent to directors of 1,178 public and 2,634 private juvenile facilities in the United States.[6] Each of the 3,812 facility directors was asked to complete the survey if the facility experienced a juvenile suicide between 1995 and 1999 (see appendix A).[7] Similar to OJJDP's *Conditions of Confinement* study (Parent et al., 1994), the project surveyed facilities that housed juveniles in more traditional types of confinement—juvenile detention centers, reception centers, training schools, ranches, camps, and farms—operated by state and local governments and private organizations.[8] Excluded from the project were open, physically unrestricted residential programs for juveniles such as shelters, halfway houses, and group homes.

To more accurately count the number of juvenile suicides in confinement between 1995 and 1999, survey forms and cover letters were also sent to the department of juvenile corrections, attorney general's office, and state medical examiner in each state; members of the National Association of Child Advocates in 47 states; child fatality review programs in 12 states; and various other state agencies (e.g., child ombudsman, licensing and regulatory services). Further, survey forms and cover letters were sent to each of OJJDP's state advisory groups, state criminal justice councils, and state juvenile justice specialists. Finally, a newspaper clipping service was used to verify juvenile suicides not identified through these more traditional sources.

The initial phase identified 110 juvenile suicides occurring between 1995 and 1999. The suicides were distributed among 38 states. Table 1 provides a breakdown of data collection sources for the suicides. Nearly half (54) of the deaths were identified from self-reporting of the juvenile facilities. Data obtained from state departments of juvenile corrections yielded an additional 27 suicides not identified through self-reporting. Of the remaining deaths, 14 were identified through other state agencies (i.e., those responsible for licensing and regulatory services), 10 through newspaper articles, and 5 through other sources (i.e., the project director's expert witness consultation and/or technical assistance to facilities that sustained these deaths). It should be noted that self-reporting was given the primary recognition for the identification of juvenile suicides. For example, if a juvenile suicide was identified by more than one source, including a self-report from the facility where the death occurred, the source would be attributed to a self-report (table 1).

Table 1: Sources Used To Identify the Number of Juvenile Suicides in Confinement, 1995–1999

Source*	N	%
Facility self-report	54	49.1
State departments of juvenile corrections	27	24.6
Other state agencies	14	12.7
Newspaper articles	10	9.1
Other sources	5	4.5
Total	**110**	**100.0**

* Each suicide is only listed once (under the highest ranking source).

Of the 54 suicides self-reported from facility directors, 26 (48.2 percent) of these deaths were unknown to any state agency (i.e., state departments of juvenile corrections or other state agencies responsible for licensing and regulatory services). Further, the 15 suicides that were identified through newspaper articles or other sources were also unknown to any state agency. Therefore, 41 (37.3 percent) of the 110 juvenile suicides identified in this study were unknown to any state agency. Most of these suicides occurred in either county detention centers or private residential treatment centers.

Phase 2

Once facilities that had experienced a suicide during the 5-year study period were identified, the second phase of the survey process was initiated. It included dissemination of a 7-page survey instrument to the directors of the facilities that sustained suicides (see appendix B). The survey instrument was designed to collect data on the following three types of characteristics:

❖ **Demographic characteristics** included age, sex, race, living arrangement, current offense(s), prior offense(s), legal status (detained, committed, other), length of confinement, drug/alcohol intoxication at confinement, history of room confinement, substance abuse history, medical/mental health history, physical/sexual abuse history, and history of suicidal behavior.

❖ **Incident characteristics** included date, time, and location of suicide; housing assignment (e.g., single or multiple occupancy); room confinement status; method and instrument used; time span between incident and finding victim; and possible precipitating factors to the suicide.

❖ **Facility characteristics** included facility type, facility ownership (e.g., state, county, private), capacity/population at time of suicide, and suicide prevention components in use (written policy, intake screening, staff training in suicide prevention and cardiopulmonary resuscitation, observation levels, safe housing, and mortality review).

The phase 2 survey instruments and cover letters were mailed to directors of the 83 facilities that sustained the 110 suicides. The process was implemented in August 2000 and initially resulted in the completion and return of 23 surveys (20.9 percent). Subsequent followup letters and telephone contact with facility directors not responding to initial survey requests occurred in October 2000, December 2000, and February 2001.[9] These efforts resulted in the completion and return of an additional 52 surveys (47.2 percent). A final request letter by OJJDP and the National Juvenile Detention Association in June 2001 resulted in an additional 4 completed surveys (3.6 percent). Respondents provided completed surveys on 79 suicides. The response rate (71.8 percent) was lower than that found in the project director's two previous national studies of jail suicide (82 percent for a 1981 study, 85 percent for a 1988 study). Several reasons were cited by juvenile facility directors for not fully participating in the study, including litigation and advice from legal counsel, sensitivity of the subject matter, issues of confidentiality, lack of time, and manpower constraints. Although 30 (27 percent) of the 110 suicides occurred in private facilities, many of which were residential treatment centers, approximately two-thirds (67 percent) of nonresponses to survey requests came from private facilities.

Findings

Project staff analyzed data on 79 suicides that occurred in public and private juvenile facilities between 1995 and 1999. The findings are presented in relationship to facility type, with 33 (41.8 percent) of the suicides having occurred in training school/secure facilities, 29 (36.7 percent) in detention centers, 12 (15.2 percent) in residential treatment centers, and 5 (6.3 percent) in reception/diagnostic centers. Almost half (48.1 percent) the suicides occurred in facilities administered by state agencies, 39.2 percent took place in county facilities, and 12.7 percent in private programs. The 79 suicides were distributed among 70 juvenile facilities: 65 facilities sustained a single suicide, 3 facilities had 2 suicides each, 1 facility had 3 suicides, and 1 facility had 5 suicides during the survey period.

Personal Characteristics of the Victims

Race

More than two-thirds (68.4 percent) of victims were Caucasian (table 2). This is not surprising given that this racial group represents more than 90 percent of suicides that occur each year in the community (Arias et al., 2003). A previous study found that Caucasian youth held in detention attempted suicide at a rate approximately 3.5 times that of African American youth (Kempton and Forehand, 1992). Although African American and Hispanic youth comprised approximately 39 percent and 18 percent, respectively, of the confined juvenile population throughout the country (Sickmund and Wan, 2001),[10] they represented only 11.4 percent and 6.3 percent of victims in this study. Caucasian and American Indian youth, on the other hand, comprised approximately 38 percent and 2 percent, respectively, of the confined juvenile population throughout the country, but 68.4 percent and 11.4 percent of victims in this study. The causes of these disproportionate relationships were outside the purview of this analysis.

Table 2: Suicides in Juvenile Facilities, 1995–1999, by Victim's Race and Facility Type

Race	Detention Center	Training School / Secure Facility	Reception / Diagnostic Center	Residential Treatment Center	Combined	
					N	%
Caucasian	17	25	3	9	54	68.4
African American	6	1	1	1	9	11.4
American Indian	3	5	0	1	9	11.4
Hispanic	2	1	1	1	5	6.3
Other	1	1	0	0	2	2.5
Total	29	33	5	12	79	100.0

Sex

The vast majority (79.7 percent) of victims were male (table 3). Given that more than 80 percent of all confined juveniles throughout the country are male (Sickmund and Wan, 2001), these findings were not surprising.

Table 3: Suicides in Juvenile Facilities, 1995–1999, by Victim's Sex and Facility Type

Sex	Detention Center	Training School / Secure Facility	Reception / Diagnostic Center	Residential Treatment Center	Combined	
					N	%
Male	23	27	5	8	63	79.7
Female	6	6	0	4	16	20.3
Total	**29**	**33**	**5**	**12**	**79**	**100.0**

Age

More than 70 percent of victims were between the ages of 15 and 17 (table 4). The average (mean) age was 15.7. The youngest victim was 12 and the oldest 20. These findings were also consistent with CJRP data (Sickmund and Wan, 2001).

Table 4: Suicides in Juvenile Facilities, 1995–1999, by Victim's Age and Facility Type

Age	Detention Center	Training School / Secure Facility	Reception / Diagnostic Center	Residential Treatment Center	Combined	
					N	%
12	1	0	0	0	1	1.3
13	0	1	0	2	3	3.8
14	5	6	0	1	12	15.2
15	10	6	2	5	23	29.1
16	3	8	3	1	15	19.0
17	9	6	0	3	18	22.8
18	1	4	0	0	5	6.3
19	0	1	0	0	1	1.3
20	0	1	0	0	1	1.3
Total	**29**	**33**	**5**	**12**	**79**	**100.0**

Note: Percents for details do not total 100.0 because of rounding.

Living Arrangement Before Confinement

More than a third (38.0 percent) of suicide victims were living with one parent at the time of their confinement (table 5). Slightly less than one quarter (22.8 percent) of victims were living with both parents.

Table 5: Suicides in Juvenile Facilities, 1995–1999, by Victim's Living Arrangement (Before Confinement) and Facility Type

Living Arrangement	Detention Center	Training School / Secure Facility	Reception / Diagnostic Center	Residential Treatment Center	Combined	
					N	%
One parent	13	10	3	4	30	38.0
Both parents	7	8	1	2	18	22.8
Community placement	3	4	0	2	9	11.4
Other relatives	3	3	0	1	7	8.9
Foster parent/guardian	2	3	0	1	6	7.6
Adoptive parents	0	3	0	1	4	5.1
Self only	0	1	0	1	2	2.5
Unknown	1	1	1	0	3	3.8
Total	**29**	**33**	**5**	**12**	**79**	**100.0**

Note: Percents for details do not total 100.0 because of rounding.

Most Serious Offense[11]

Most (69.6 percent) victims were confined on nonviolent (i.e., nonperson) offenses, with property offenses accounting for the highest percentage (32.9 percent) of victims (table 6). In addition, the public order, status, and probation violation categories combined represented more than a third (34.2 percent) of the offenses. Person offenses accounted for 30.4 percent of victims, and only 2.5 percent of victims were confined on drug offenses. Approximately 40 percent (13 of 33) of victims housed in a training school/secure facility were confined for a person offense.

With only a slight variance, these findings were consistent with data on the confined juvenile population. For example, person offenses accounted for 35 percent and property offenses accounted for 29 percent of confined juveniles (Sickmund and Wan, 2001). However, whereas the public order, status, and probation violation categories combined represented 27 percent of confined juveniles, these categories represented 34.2 percent of victims in this study.

Table 6: Suicides in Juvenile Facilities, 1995–1999, by Victim's Most Serious Offense and Facility Type

Most Serious Offense	Detention Center	Training School / Secure Facility	Reception / Diagnostic Center	Residential Treatment Center	Combined	
					N	%
Property	11	10	2	3	26	32.9
Person	8	13	2	1	24	30.4
Status	2	4	0	4	10	12.7
Probation violation	6	2	0	1	9	11.4
Public order	2	3	1	2	8	10.1
Drug	0	1	0	1	2	2.5
Total	29	33	5	12	79	100.0

Additional Charges

At confinement, 39.2 percent of victims had a second charge. Property offenses accounted for the majority (51.7 percent) of additional charges, followed by person offenses (19.4 percent). The public order, status, and probation violation categories combined represented 28.9 percent of the second charges at confinement.

Confinement Status

Approximately two-thirds (67.1 percent) of victims were being held on commitment status at time of death (table 7). This finding was significantly different from a national study on jail suicides that found the overwhelming majority of victims were on detention status at time of death (Hayes, 1989). The finding was, however, somewhat consistent with national data on confined juveniles throughout the country that found 74 percent of youth were on commitment status (Sickmund and Wan, 2001). Not surprisingly, the vast majority (79.3 percent) of victims held in detention centers were on detention status and all training school/secure facility victims were on commitment status at time of death.

Table 7: Suicides in Juvenile Facilities, 1995–1999, by Victim's Confinement Status and Facility Type

Confinement Status*	Detention Center	Training School / Secure Facility	Reception / Diagnostic Center	Residential Treatment Center	Combined N	%
Committed	6	33	5	9	53	67.1
Detained	23	0	0	3	26	32.9
Total	29	33	5	12	79	100.0

* Committed juveniles included those placed in a facility as part of a court-ordered disposition. Detained juveniles included those held awaiting a court hearing, adjudication, disposition, and/or placement.

Most Serious Prior Offenses

A significant majority (62 of 79, or 78.5 percent) of suicide victims had a history of prior offenses within the juvenile justice system (table 8). Of victims who had a history of prior offenses, most committed crimes of a nonviolent nature, with property offenses the most common (50.0 percent). Public order, status, and probation violation categories combined represented 22.5 percent of the most serious prior offenses; person offenses accounted for 22.6 percent of victims' prior offenses.

Table 8: Suicides in Juvenile Facilities by Victims With Prior Offenses, 1995–1999, by Victim's Most Serious Prior Offense and Facility Type

Most Serious Prior Offense	Detention Center	Training School / Secure Facility	Reception / Diagnostic Center	Residential Treatment Center	Combined N	%
Property	12	13	1	5	31	50.0
Person	5	9	0	0	14	22.6
Status	5	4	0	2	11	17.7
Public order	1	1	0	0	2	3.2
Probation violation	0	1	0	0	1	1.6
Drug	0	0	0	0	0	0.0
Unknown	1	0	1	1	3	4.8
Total	24	28	2	8	62	100.0

Note: Percents for details do not total 100.0 because of rounding.

Length of Confinement (Before Suicide)

Relatively few (3.8 percent) juvenile suicides occurred within the first 24 hours of confinement, and all these deaths occurred in detention centers (table 9). This finding significantly differed from a national study on jail suicides that found more than half took place within the first 24 hours, with almost a third occurring within the first 3 hours (Hayes, 1989). Instead, the deaths in this national survey of juvenile suicide in confinement were distributed fairly evenly during a more than 12-month period. For example, the same number of suicides (13) occurred within the first 3 days of confinement as occurred in more than 10 months of confinement.[12] The majority of suicides (31.7 percent) occurred within 1 to 4 months of confinement. However, all the detention center suicides occurred within the first 4 months of confinement, with more than 40 percent occurring within the first 72 hours, while most (72.7 percent) training school/secure facility suicides occurred 3 months or more following confinement.[13]

Table 9: Suicides in Juvenile Facilities, 1995–1999, by Victim's Length of Confinement (Before Suicide) and Facility Type

Length of Confinement	Detention Center	Training School / Secure Facility	Reception / Diagnostic Center	Residential Treatment Center	Combined N	Combined %
Less than 24 hours	3	0	0	0	3	3.8
1–3 days	9	0	0	1	10	12.7
4–6 days	3	0	0	0	3	3.8
7–13 days	3	3	0	0	6	7.6
14–30 days	4	2	1	1	8	10.1
1–2 months	4	4	3	2	13	16.5
3–4 months	3	7	0	2	12	15.2
5–6 months	0	4	0	3	7	8.9
7–9 months	0	2	1	1	4	5.1
10–12 months	0	1	0	2	3	3.8
More than 12 months	0	10	0	0	10	12.7
Total	**29**	**33**	**5**	**12**	**79**	**100.0**

Note: Percents for details do not total 100.0 because of rounding.

Substance Abuse

Nearly three-quarters (73.4 percent) of victims had a history of substance abuse (table 10). Approximately one-third (32.8 percent) of these victims used alcohol, marijuana, or cocaine before confinement. This finding is consistent with data suggesting that two-thirds of confined youth have one or more alcohol, drug, or mental disorders (Teplin et al., 2002). The victim's history of substance abuse was unknown in a number of cases, with detention centers accounting for most (11 of 13) nonresponses.

Table 10: Suicides in Juvenile Facilities, 1995–1999, by Victim's History of Substance Abuse and Facility Type

History of Substance Abuse	Detention Center	Training School / Secure Facility	Reception / Diagnostic Center	Residential Treatment Center	Combined N	Combined %
Yes	15	29	5	9	58	73.4
No	3	2	0	3	8	10.1
Unknown	11	2	0	0	13	16.5
Total	**29**	**33**	**5**	**12**	**79**	**100.0**

Medical Problems

Most (64.5 percent) victims did not have a history of medical problems (table 11). Allergies and asthma were common types of medical problems found in the few victims who had problems. Detention centers accounted for most (10 of 13) nonresponses.

Table 11: Suicides in Juvenile Facilities, 1995–1999, by Victim's History of Medical Problems and Facility Type

History of Medical Problems	Detention Center	Training School / Secure Facility	Reception / Diagnostic Center	Residential Treatment Center	Combined N	Combined %
Yes	5	9	1	0	15	19.0
No	14	23	4	10	51	64.5
Unknown	10	1	0	2	13	16.5
Total	**29**	**33**	**5**	**12**	**79**	**100.0**

Emotional Abuse

Somewhat less than half the victims had a history of emotional abuse (table 12). The most frequent examples were excessive punishment, neglect and/or abandonment, verbal abuse, and other types of family dysfunction. The victim's history of emotional abuse was unknown in almost one-quarter of the cases, with detention centers accounting for more than half the nonresponses (10 of 19).

Table 12: Suicides in Juvenile Facilities, 1995–1999, by Victim's History of Emotional Abuse and Facility Type

History of Emotional Abuse	Detention Center	Training School / Secure Facility	Reception / Diagnostic Center	Residential Treatment Center	Combined N	Combined %
Yes	11	15	2	7	35	44.3
No	8	12	2	3	25	31.6
Unknown	10	6	1	2	19	24.1
Total	29	33	5	12	79	100.0

Physical Abuse

Slightly more than a third of victims had a history of physical abuse (table 13), with an immediate family member (e.g., father or stepfather) being the perpetrator of the abuse in the majority of cases (20 of 27). Again, the survey revealed a considerable percentage of unknown responses to this variable, with detention centers providing almost half (8 of 17) the nonresponses.

Table 13: Suicides in Juvenile Facilities, 1995–1999, by Victim's History of Physical Abuse and Facility Type

History of Physical Abuse	Detention Center	Training School / Secure Facility	Reception / Diagnostic Center	Residential Treatment Center	Combined N	Combined %
Yes	7	15	1	4	27	34.2
No	14	13	2	6	35	44.3
Unknown	8	5	2	2	17	21.5
Total	29	33	5	12	79	100.0

Sexual Abuse

More than a quarter of victims had a history of sexual abuse, with an equal number of victims whose history of sexual abuse was unknown (table 14). For those who were abused, an immediate family member (e.g., father or stepfather) was the perpetrator in many cases. Detention centers accounted for half the nonresponses.

Table 14: Suicides in Juvenile Facilities, 1995–1999, by Victim's History of Sexual Abuse and Facility Type

History of Sexual Abuse	Detention Center	Training School / Secure Facility	Reception / Diagnostic Center	Residential Treatment Center	Combined N	Combined %
Yes	3	12	3	4	22	27.8
No	15	14	1	5	35	44.3
Unknown	11	7	1	3	22	27.8
Total	29	33	5	12	79	100.0

Note: Percents for details do not total 100.0 because of rounding.

Mental Illness

Nearly two-thirds (65.8 percent) of victims had a history of mental illness, with many (65.3 percent) of these victims suffering from depression at time of death. Other mental illnesses reported included attention deficit/hyperactivity disorder, conduct disorder, post-traumatic stress disorder, and psychotic disorder (53.5 percent of the victims were taking psychotropic medication at the time of their death).[14] Although earlier research also indicates that a significant percentage of youth in the juvenile justice system suffer from at least one mental disorder and have higher rates of mental disorders than youth in the general population (Cocozza and Skowyra, 2000), it should be noted that substance abuse disorder (which accounts for a sizable percentage of psychiatric disorders) was not included in this category. Detention centers accounted for all nonresponses.

Table 15: Suicides in Juvenile Facilities, 1995–1999, by Victim's History of Mental Illness and Facility Type

History of Mental Illness	Detention Center	Training School / Secure Facility	Reception / Diagnostic Center	Residential Treatment Center	Combined N	%
Yes	14	23	4	11	52	65.8
No	6	10	1	1	18	22.8
Unknown	9	0	0	0	9	11.4
Total	29	33	5	12	79	100.0

Prior Suicidal Behavior

More than two-thirds (69.6 percent) of victims had a history of suicidal behavior (table 16). The most frequent type of suicidal behavior was suicide attempts (45.5 percent), followed by suicidal ideation/threat (30.9 percent), and suicidal gesture/self-mutilation (23.6 percent). Although other research, summarized earlier in this report, shows that a notable percentage (varying between 8 percent and 52 percent) of confined youth had a history of suicidal behavior, the finding from this national survey suggests that confined youth who commit suicide have a higher percentage of prior suicidal behavior than those confined youth who engage in suicidal behavior but do not commit suicide. Compared with other facility types, suicide victims in detention centers were less likely to have a known history of suicidal behavior (only 51.7 percent, as compared with 80.0 percent in all other facilities).

Table 16: Suicides in Juvenile Facilities, 1995–1999, by Victim's Prior Suicidal Behavior and Facility Type

Prior Suicidal Behavior	Detention Center	Training School / Secure Facility	Reception / Diagnostic Center	Residential Treatment Center	Combined N	%
Yes	15	26	5	9	55	69.6
No	12	7	0	3	22	27.8
Unknown	2	0	0	0	2	2.5
Total	29	33	5	12	79	100.0

Note: Percents for details do not total 100.0 because of rounding.

History of Room Confinement

For purposes of this study, room confinement was defined as a "behavioral sanction imposed on youth that restricted movement for varying amounts of time." It included, but was not limited to, isolation, segregation, time-out, or a quiet room. Room confinement did not include youth assigned to their room during traditional nonwaking hours.

Most (62.0 percent) suicide victims had a history of room confinement (table 17). The circumstances that led to room confinement included threat or actual physical abuse of staff or peers (40.5 percent), verbal abuse of staff or peers (26.2 percent), failure to follow program rules or inappropriate behavior (26.2 percent), and other (7.1 percent), which included two cases of youth involved in gang activity and one case of a standard protocol for new intake.

Table 17: Suicides in Juvenile Facilities, 1995–1999, by Victim's History of Room Confinement and Facility Type

History of Room Confinement	Detention Center	Training School / Secure Facility	Reception / Diagnostic Center	Residential Treatment Center	Combined	
					N	%
Yes	18	20	3	8	49	62.0
No	11	13	2	4	30	38.0
Total	29	33	5	12	79	100.0

Suicide Incident Characteristics

Date

Table 18 shows the distribution of juvenile suicides during the 5-year study period (1995–1999). The fact that 1997 accounted for the highest number (and 1995 the lowest number) of suicides was not statistically significant. For example, the reporting of only 9 suicides during 1995 may have more to do with the inability of respondents to collect data that was several years old or the possibility that, given high staff turnover in many facilities, survey respondents were not employed at the facility when the earlier suicides took place.

Table 18: Suicides in Juvenile Facilities, 1995–1999, by Year of Suicide and Facility Type

Year	Detention Center	Training School / Secure Facility	Reception / Diagnostic Center	Residential Treatment Center	Combined	
					N	%
1995	4	3	0	2	9	11.4
1996	3	11	1	1	16	20.3
1997	10	6	2	4	22	27.8
1998	6	8	1	3	18	22.8
1999	6	5	1	2	14	17.7
Total	29	33	5	12	79	100.0

Suicides were distributed throughout the year, although more than 30 percent of the reported deaths occurred in the months of January and May. Contrary to common belief, certain seasons of the year and holidays did not correlate with a higher number of suicides. Further, no statistically significant difference existed regarding the day of the week on which the suicides occurred.

Time

Research on adult jail suicide has found that deaths are more prevalent when staff supervision is reduced. For example, less than 20 percent of deaths in a national study of jail suicides occurred during the 6-hour period between 9 a.m. and 3 p.m., a major portion of the day shift (Hayes, 1989). Findings from this study indicate that most (70.9 percent) suicides occurred during traditional waking hours (6 a.m. to 9 p.m.), while 29.1 percent occurred during traditional nonwaking hours (9 p.m. to 6 a.m.) (table

19). In addition, approximately half (50.6 percent) the suicides occurred during the 6-hour period between 6 p.m. and midnight, and almost a third (29.1 percent) occurred between 6 p.m. and 9 p.m.

Table 19: Suicides in Juvenile Facilities, 1995–1999, by Time of Suicide and Facility Type

Time of Suicide	Detention Center	Training School / Secure Facility	Reception / Diagnostic Center	Residential Treatment Center	Combined	
					N	%
12 midnight to 3 a.m.	1	2	0	0	3	3.8
3 a.m. to 6 a.m.	1	1	0	1	3	3.8
6 a.m. to 9 a.m.	1	1	1	0	3	3.8
9 a.m. to 12 noon	5	5	0	1	11	13.9
12 noon to 3 p.m.	2	3	1	1	7	8.9
3 p.m. to 6 p.m.	5	5	0	2	12	15.2
6 p.m. to 9 p.m.	8	9	2	4	23	29.1
9 p.m. to 12 midnight	6	7	1	3	17	21.5
Total	29	33	5	12	79	100.0

Method, Instrument, and Anchoring Device

The study found that all but one victim (98.7 percent) used hanging as the method of suicide (table 20). (The sole victim of other means absconded from the facility and ran in front of a passing train.) The vast majority (71.8 percent) of victims used bedding (e.g., sheet, blanket) as the instrument to hang themselves. Clothing, excluding belts and shoelaces, was used to a lesser degree. Other instruments included a towel and a bag.

Table 20: Suicides by Hanging in Juvenile Facilities, 1995–1999, by Instrument Used and Facility Type

Instrument	Detention Center	Training School / Secure Facility	Reception / Diagnostic Center	Residential Treatment Center	Combined	
					N	%
Bedding	23	22	3	8	56	71.8
Clothing	5	4	0	1	10	12.8
Belt	1	1	0	2	4	5.1
Shoelace	0	3	1	0	4	5.1
Other	0	2	1	1	4	5.1
Total	29	32	5	12	78	100.0

Note: Percents for details do not total 100.0 because of rounding.

Suicide victims used a variety of anchoring devices, including door hinges/knobs, air vents, bedframes, and window frames (table 21). Other devices included toilets, sinks, and television stands.

Table 21: Suicides by Hanging in Juvenile Facilities, 1995–1999, by Anchoring Device Used and Facility Type

Anchoring Device	Detention Center	Training School / Secure Facility	Reception / Diagnostic Center	Residential Treatment Center	Combined	
					N	%
Door hinge/knob	6	6	0	4	16	20.5
Air vent	7	6	2	0	15	19.2
Bedframe	7	5	1	2	15	19.2
Window frame	6	5	0	0	11	14.1
Closet rod	0	2	1	4	7	9.0
Sprinkler head	2	3	0	1	6	7.7
Other	1	3	1	1	6	7.7
Unknown	0	2	0	0	2	2.6
Total	29	32	5	12	78	100.0

Intoxication

None of the 79 victims was under the influence of alcohol or drugs at the time of suicide. This finding is in stark contrast to a national study on jail suicides that found more than 60 percent of adult suicide victims were intoxicated at the time of their suicide (Hayes, 1989).

Room Assignment

At the time of the suicide, the data indicate that most (74.7 percent) victims were assigned to single occupancy rooms, while a quarter (25.3 percent) were assigned to multiple occupancy rooms. No significant differences between room assignments and the types of facilities where the suicides occurred were noted.

Time Span

Approximately 41 percent of respondents stated that staff found the victim in less than 15 minutes following the last observation of the youth (table 22). However, slightly more than 15 percent of victims were reported to be found more than an hour following last observation, including several victims found after 3 hours. In one case, the time span between the last observation and the suicide was unknown.

Table 22: Suicides in Juvenile Facilities, 1995–1999, by Time Span Between Last Observation and Finding Victim and Facility Type

Time Span	Detention Center	Training School / Secure Facility	Reception / Diagnostic Center	Residential Treatment Center	Combined	
					N	%
Less than 15 minutes	14	9	1	8	32	40.5
15–30 minutes	6	14	2	1	23	29.1
31–60 minutes	5	2	2	2	11	13.9
1–3 hours	2	5	0	0	7	8.9
More than 3 hours	2	3	0	0	5	6.3
Unknown	0	0	0	1	1	1.3
Total	29	33	5	12	79	100.0

Room Confinement

Approximately half (50.6 percent) the victims were on room confinement status at time of death (table 23).[15] As previously indicated, room confinement was defined as a behavioral sanction imposed on youth that restricted movement for varying amounts of time. Room confinement did not include youth assigned to their room during traditional nonwaking hours (9 p.m. to 6 a.m.). Compared to other facility types, a much smaller percentage (16.7 percent) of suicide victims housed in residential treatment centers were on room confinement status at time of death.

Table 23: Suicides in Juvenile Facilities, 1995–1999, by Victim's Room Confinement Status and Facility Type

Room Confinement	Detention Center	Training School / Secure Facility	Reception / Diagnostic Center	Residential Treatment Center	Combined	
					N	%
Yes	16	18	4	2	40	50.6
No	13	15	1	10	39	49.4
Total	29	33	5	12	79	100.0

In addition, 85.0 percent of victims who committed suicide while on room confinement died during waking hours (6 a.m. to 9 p.m.), a rate higher than that of victims who committed suicide during waking hours but who were not on room confinement status (70.9 percent).

Suicide Precaution Status

A relatively small percentage (16.5 percent) of youth were on suicide precaution status at time of death (table 24). Of the 13 victims on suicide precaution status, 10 were required to be observed at 15-minute intervals, the three remaining youth were to be observed at continuous, 5-minute, and 60-minute intervals, respectively. Despite their identified risk of suicide, almost half (6 of 13) these victims were last observed more than 15 minutes before their suicides.

Table 24: Suicides in Juvenile Facilities, 1995–1999, by Victim's Suicide Precaution Status and Facility Type

Suicide Precaution Status	Detention Center	Training School / Secure Facility	Reception / Diagnostic Center	Residential Treatment Center	Combined N	%
Yes	7	5	0	1	13	16.5
No	22	28	5	11	66	83.5
Total	**29**	**33**	**5**	**12**	**79**	**100.0**

Assessment by Qualified Mental Health Professional

National juvenile correctional standards and standard correctional practice indicate that confined youth should be assessed as soon as possible by a qualified mental health professional (National Commission on Correctional Health Care, 1995, 1999, 2004; Roush, 1996; Underwood and Berenson, 2001), with Performance-based Standards requiring an assessment within 7 days of entry into the facility (Council of Juvenile Correctional Administrators, 2003).[16] For purposes of this study and consistent with national standards, qualified mental health professional was defined as an individual who by virtue of his or her education, credentials, and experience is permitted by law to evaluate and care for the mental health needs of patients. This definition includes, but is not limited to, a psychiatrist, psychologist, clinical social worker, and psychiatric nurse. This examination by a qualified mental health professional is separate from an initial intake screening.

Most (69.6 percent) victims were assessed by a qualified mental health professional (table 25). Compared to other facility types, a smaller percentage (34.5 percent) of suicide victims housed in detention centers received mental health assessments. However, slightly more than half (51.7 percent) the detention center victims committed suicide within the first 6 days of confinement (see table 9), possibly precluding the opportunity for assessment.

Table 25: Suicides in Juvenile Facilities, 1995–1999, by Victim's Assessment by a Qualified Mental Health Professional (QMHP) and Facility Type

QMHP Assessment	Detention Center	Training School / Secure Facility	Reception / Diagnostic Center	Residential Treatment Center	Combined N	%
Yes	10	29	5	11	55	69.6
No	19	4	0	1	24	30.4
Total	**29**	**33**	**5**	**12**	**79**	**100.0**

Almost half (49.1 percent) the victims receiving a mental health assessment had a contact visit with a qualified mental health professional within 6 days of death (table 26). However, the data also showed that 20.0 percent of assessed victims had not been assessed within 30 days of death, suggesting that slightly less than half (44.3 percent) the victims in the study either had never been assessed by a qualified mental health professional or had not been assessed within 30 days of death.

Table 26: Suicides in Juvenile Facilities by Victims Who Were Assessed by a Qualified Mental Health Professional (QMHP), 1995–1999, by Time of Victim's Last Contact With QMHP and Facility Type

Last Contact With QMHP	Detention Center	Training School / Secure Facility	Reception / Diagnostic Center	Residential Treatment Center	Combined	
					N	%
Less than 24 hours	2	3	1	3	9	16.4
1–3 days	5	3	1	3	12	21.8
4–6 days	1	4	0	1	6	10.9
7–13 days	0	8	2	2	12	21.8
14–30 days	1	3	0	1	5	9.1
1–2 months	1	2	0	0	3	5.5
3–4 months	0	0	0	0	0	0.0
5–6 months	0	1	0	0	1	1.8
7–9 months	0	1	0	0	1	1.8
10–12 months	0	1	0	1	2	3.6
More than 12 months	0	3	1	0	4	7.3
Total	10	29	5	11	55	100.0

Juvenile Facility Characteristics

Facility Type and Population

As previously indicated, this national survey of juvenile suicides in confinement found that 41.8 percent of the juvenile suicides took place in training school/secure facilities, 36.7 percent occurred in detention centers, 15.2 percent in residential treatment centers, and 6.3 percent in reception/diagnostic centers. In addition, almost half (48.1 percent) the suicides occurred in facilities administered by state agencies, 39.2 percent took place in county facilities, and 12.7 percent in private programs. Two-thirds (67.1 percent) occurred in facilities with populations of 200 or fewer youth, and 41.8 percent occurred in facilities with 50 or fewer youth (table 27).[17] The study did not find any evidence to suggest that overcrowding was a contributing factor to juvenile suicide. In fact, some two-thirds (67.6 percent) of suicides took place in facilities that were at or below bed capacity, with an additional 9.5 percent of suicides occurring in facilities that were slightly (less than 10 percent) over capacity.

Table 27: Suicides in Juvenile Facilities, 1995–1999, by Population of Facility and Facility Type

Facility Population	Detention Center	Training School / Secure Facility	Reception / Diagnostic Center	Residential Treatment Center	Combined	
					N	%
50 or fewer youth	20	4	1	8	33	41.8
51–200 youth	7	9	2	2	20	25.3
201–500 youth	1	11	1	0	13	16.5
501–1,000 youth	0	7	0	0	7	8.9
More than 1,000 youth	0	1	0	0	1	1.3
Unknown	1	1	1	2	5	6.3
Total	29	33	5	12	79	100.0

Note: Percents for details do not total 100.0 because of rounding.

Written Suicide Prevention Policy

National juvenile correctional standards and standard correctional practice indicate that juvenile facilities should have a written suicide prevention policy that details the identification and management of suicidal youth (American Correctional Association, 1991; Council of Juvenile Correctional Administrators, 2003; Hayes, 1999; National Commission on Correctional Health Care, 1995, 1999, 2004; Roush, 1996). The vast majority (78.5 percent) of suicides occurred in facilities that maintained a written suicide prevention policy at the time of the suicide (table 28), although this was less true for suicides that took place in detention centers (62.1 percent).

Table 28: Suicides in Juvenile Facilities, 1995–1999, by Facility's Maintenance of a Written Suicide Prevention Policy and Facility Type

Written Suicide Prevention Policy	Detention Center	Training School / Secure Facility	Reception / Diagnostic Center	Residential Treatment Center	Combined	
					N	%
Yes	18	30	4	10	62	78.5
No	11	3	1	2	17	21.5
Total	29	33	5	12	79	100.0

Intake Screening for Suicide Risk

Most (70.9 percent) suicides took place in facilities that maintained an intake screening process to identify suicide risk of youth entering the facility (table 29), although this was true for less than half (48.3 percent) the suicides in detention centers. This finding is consistent with other OJJDP data suggesting that approximately 70 percent of confined youth are screened for suicide risk (OJJDP, 2002).

Table 29: Suicides in Juvenile Facilities, 1995–1999, by Intake Screening of Victim for Suicide Risk and Facility Type

Intake Screening	Detention Center	Training School / Secure Facility	Reception / Diagnostic Center	Residential Treatment Center	Combined	
					N	%
Yes	14	29	5	8	56	70.9
No	15	4	0	4	23	29.1
Total	29	33	5	12	79	100.0

Suicide Prevention Training

More than half (57.0 percent) the juvenile suicides occurred in facilities that provided some type of suicide prevention training (pre-service, annual, or periodic) to direct care staff (table 30).

Table 30: Suicides in Juvenile Facilities, 1995–1999, by Facility's Provision of Suicide Prevention Training and Facility Type

Suicide Prevention Training	Detention Center	Training School / Secure Facility	Reception / Diagnostic Center	Residential Treatment Center	Combined	
					N	%
Yes	16	19	4	6	45	57.0
No	13	14	1	6	34	43.0
Total	29	33	5	12	79	100.0

Of the 45 suicides that occurred in facilities that provided suicide prevention training, two-thirds (66.7 percent) were in facilities that provided annual instruction (table 31), with training schools/secure facilities providing the lowest percentage (42.1 percent) of annual training. Only 37.9 percent (30 of 79) of the suicides took place in facilities that provided annual suicide prevention training to their direct care staff.

Table 31: Suicides in Juvenile Facilities That Provide Suicide Prevention Training, 1995–1999, by Frequency of (Annual) Training and Facility Type

Annual Suicide Prevention Training	Detention Center	Training School / Secure Facility	Reception / Diagnostic Center	Residential Treatment Center	Combined	
					N	%
Yes	13	8	4	5	30	66.7
No	3	11	0	1	15	33.3
Total	16	19	4	6	45	100.0

Approximately half (51.1 percent) the suicides in facilities that provided suicide prevention training were in facilities that provided the training in a 1- or 2-hour block (table 32). Only 3 suicides took place in a facility that provided a full day (7–8 hours) of instruction.

Table 32: Suicides in Juvenile Facilities That Provide Suicide Prevention Training, 1995–1999, by Duration of Training and Facility Type

Duration of Suicide Prevention Training	Detention Center	Training School / Secure Facility	Reception / Diagnostic Center	Residential Treatment Center	Combined	
					N	%
1–2 hours	11	8	2	2	23	51.1
3–4 hours	3	1	2	1	7	15.6
5–6 hours	0	1	0	1	2	4.4
7–8 hours	1	2	0	0	3	6.7
Unknown	1	7	0	2	10	22.2
Total	16	19	4	6	45	100.0

Certification in Cardiopulmonary Resuscitation

Most (68.4 percent) suicides occurred in facilities where all direct care staff had received certification in cardiopulmonary resuscitation (CPR) (table 33), although this was true to a lesser degree (54.5 percent) in training schools/secure facilities.

Table 33: Suicides in Juvenile Facilities, 1995–1999, by Staff Certification in Cardiopulmonary Resuscitation (CPR) and Facility Type

Staff Certification in CPR	Detention Center	Training School / Secure Facility	Reception / Diagnostic Center	Residential Treatment Center	Combined	
					N	%
Yes	23	18	4	9	54	68.4
No	6	15	1	3	25	31.6
Total	29	33	5	12	79	100.0

Suicide Precaution Protocol

The overwhelming majority (90.0 percent) of victims were located in facilities that maintained a suicide precaution protocol for the observation of youth (excluding closed-circuit television monitoring) at time of suicide (table 34).

Table 34: Suicides in Juvenile Facilities, 1995–1999, by Facility's Maintenance of a Suicide Precaution Protocol and Facility Type

Suicide Prevention Protocol	Detention Center	Training School / Secure Facility	Reception / Diagnostic Center	Residential Treatment Center	Combined	
					N	%
Yes	25	32	5	9	71	90.0
No	4	1	0	3	8	10.0
Total	29	33	5	12	79	100.0

Of these 71 victims, less than half (47.9 percent) were in facilities where constant observation was the highest level of suicide precaution in the facility, including only 28.0 percent of suicides in detention centers (table 35). A sizable number (36.6 percent) were in facilities that reported observation at 15-minute intervals as the highest suicide precaution level.

Table 35: Suicides in Juvenile Facilities That Maintain a Suicide Prevention Protocol, 1995–1999, by Highest Frequency Level of Observation and Facility Type

Highest Frequency Level of Observation	Detention Center	Training School / Secure Facility	Reception / Diagnostic Center	Residential Treatment Center	Combined	
					N	%
Constant	7	18	3	6	34	47.9
Every 5 minutes	3	1	1	2	7	9.9
Every 10 minutes	0	1	0	0	1	1.4
Every 15 minutes	12	12	1	1	26	36.6
Every 30 minutes	2	0	0	0	2	2.8
Unknown	1	0	0	0	1	1.4
Total	25	32	5	9	71	100.0

Safe Housing

Less than half (45.6 percent) the suicides occurred in a facility that had a housing process by which a suicidal youth would be assigned to a safe and protrusion-free room (table 36). Although the majority (60.5 percent) of suicides in training schools/secure facilities and reception/diagnostic centers took place in a facility that provided safe and protrusion-free housing for suicidal youth, this was true for only 34.5 percent of the suicides in detention facilities and 25.0 percent of the suicides in residential treatment centers.

Table 36: Suicides in Juvenile Facilities, 1995–1999, by Facility's Provision of Safe Housing for Suicidal Youth and Facility Type

Safe Housing	Detention Center	Training School / Secure Facility	Reception / Diagnostic Center	Residential Treatment Center	Combined	
					N	%
Yes	10	20	3	3	36	45.6
No	19	13	2	9	43	54.4
Total	29	33	5	12	79	100.0

Mortality Review

National juvenile correctional standards recommend that a mortality review be conducted following each suicide (Hayes, 1999; National Commission on Correctional Health Care, 1995, 1999, 2004; Roush, 1996). For purposes of this study, mortality review is defined as "a multidisciplinary committee process that examined the events surrounding the death to determine if the incident was preventable. The review process might include recommendations aimed at reducing the opportunity of future deaths." The process also attempts to identify any possible precipitating factors that may have caused the suicide.

Most (64.6 percent) respondents reported that a mortality review was conducted following the juvenile suicide (table 37), although deaths in detention centers were reviewed to a lesser degree (51.7 percent).

Table 37: Suicides in Juvenile Facilities, 1995–1999, by Mortality Review of Suicide and Facility Type

Mortality Review	Detention Center	Training School / Secure Facility	Reception / Diagnostic Center	Residential Treatment Center	Combined N	%
Yes	15	21	4	11	51	64.6
No	14	12	1	1	28	35.4
Total	29	33	5	12	79	100.0

Of the suicides that occurred in facilities that conducted mortality reviews, precipitating factors were identified for more than half (58.8 percent). These factors include:

❖ Fear of waiver to adult system, transfer to a more secure juvenile facility, or pending undesirable placement (including home) (10 cases).

❖ Recent death of a family member (6 cases).

❖ Failure in the program (5 cases).

❖ Contagion (from another recent suicide in facility) (3 cases).

❖ Parent(s) threat of/failure to visit (2 cases).

❖ Other (i.e., loss of relationship, close proximity to birthday, suicide pact with peer, ridicule from peers) (4 cases).

In several cases, more than one precipitating factor was identified—only the perceived leading factor is listed above. However, precipitating factors were offered by respondents for only 30 (38.0 percent) of the 79 suicides reported in this study.

Special Considerations

Comprehensive Suicide Prevention Programming

National juvenile correctional standards and standard correctional practice require that juvenile facilities have a written suicide prevention policy that includes a variety of components (American Correctional Association, 1991; Council of Juvenile Correctional Administrators, 2003; Hayes, 1999; National Commission on Correctional Health Care, 1995, 1999, 2004; Roush, 1996). In OJJDP's *Conditions of Confinement* study, researchers evaluating suicide prevention practices used four specific assessment criteria (written procedures, intake screening, staff training, and close observation), and found that 89 percent of juveniles were housed in facilities with a written suicide prevention plan, 72 percent were in facilities that screened juveniles for suicide risk at admission, 75 percent were in facilities where staff were trained in suicide prevention, and 50 percent were in facilities that monitored suicidal youth at least four times per hour. However, the OJJDP study found that only 25 percent of confined juveniles were in facilities that conformed to all four suicide prevention assessment criteria (Parent et al., 1994).

Although the OJJDP study could not assess the quality of each of the four criteria operating within the juvenile facilities because most data were self-reported, other findings were equally revealing. For example, facilities that conducted screening for suicide risk at admission and trained their staff in suicide prevention had lower rates of suicidal behavior among their residents than those that did not. Furthermore, although written policies to provide close observation of suicidal residents did not appear to significantly reduce the rate of suicidal behavior, they could play a role in reducing completed suicides because these policies are often implemented after the risk is recognized (Parent et al., 1994).

For this national survey of juvenile suicide in confinement, data were collected to determine whether facilities sustaining a suicide had comprehensive suicide prevention programming in place at time of death. Consistent with national juvenile correctional standards, comprehensive suicide prevention programming included the following seven critical components: written policy, intake screening, training, CPR certification, observation, safe housing, and mortality review (Hayes, 1999). The vast majority (78.5 percent) of respondents in this study indicated they had a written suicide prevention policy at time of suicide (see table 28). However, only 20.3 percent occurred in facilities that had programming encompassing all seven suicide prevention components (table 38). The degree to which suicides occurred in a facility that had all seven suicide prevention components varied considerably by facility type: detention centers (10.3 percent), training schools/secure facilities (24.2 percent), reception/diagnostic centers (40.0 percent), and residential treatment centers (25.0 percent).

Consistent with OJJDP's *Conditions of Confinement* study, these findings suggest that, although there was a higher rate of compliance with individual suicide prevention components, few facilities that sustained a suicide had all components of a comprehensive suicide prevention program.

Table 38: Suicides in Juvenile Facilities, 1995–1999, by Number of Suicide Prevention Components Implemented by the Facility and Facility Type

Suicide Prevention Components	Detention Center	Training School / Secure Facility	Reception / Diagnostic Center	Residential Treatment Center	Combined	
					N	%
0	2	0	0	0	2	2.5
1	2	0	0	1	3	3.8
2	2	3	0	1	6	7.6
3	4	2	0	1	7	8.9
4	4	7	1	3	15	19.0
5	6	5	1	1	13	16.5
6	6	8	1	2	17	21.5
7	3	8	2	3	16	20.3
Total	29	33	5	12	79	100.0

Note: Percents for details do not total 100.0 because of rounding.

Room Confinement

Isolation and segregation, terms commonly used in the adult corrections field, are rarely heard in the juvenile corrections system. Instead, isolation in a juvenile facility is often referred to as "room confinement," a term that includes time-out, quiet time, restriction, adjustment, conflict resolution, room lock, and off-program. Youth who are removed from the room in which they normally sleep are often held in seclusion, exclusion, separation, and special management. In addition, the youth of an entire housing unit may be confined to their rooms at various parts of a day.

In addition, although room confinement is often used both as a behavioral sanction resulting from assaultive or disruptive behavior and as a form of quarantine for newly arrived residents or those in need of protective custody, it is also used for suicidal youth. For example, a recent U.S. Department of Justice investigation of conditions of confinement within a state juvenile correctional system found that:

> Girls in the SIU (Special Intervention Unit) at Columbia are punished for acting out or being suicidal by being placed in a cell called the "dark room." The "dark room" is a locked, windowless isolation cell with lighting controlled by staff. When the lights are turned out, as the girls reported they are when the room is in use, the room is completely dark. The room is stripped of everything but a drain in the floor which serves as a toilet.

> Most girls are stripped naked when placed in the "dark room." According to Columbia staff, the reason girls must remove their clothing before being placed in the room is that there is metal grating on the ceiling and the cell door which could be used for hanging attempts by suicidal girls. (U.S. Department of Justice, 2003:7)

Although room confinement and isolation can be effective behavioral management tools when appropriately used for short durations that are closely monitored and clearly documented (see National Commission on Correctional Health Care, 1999, 2004), the presence of a separate isolation unit within a juvenile facility may provide an environment in which an overreliance on isolation is likely to be the primary behavior management strategy (Mitchell and Varley, 1990). Federal investigations of several juvenile corrections systems throughout the country have found both excessive and unjustified use of isolation and room confinement (*United States* v. *State of Arizona*, 2004; *United States* v. *State of Georgia*, 1998; *United States* v. *Commonwealth of Kentucky*, 1995; *United States* v. *State of Louisiana*,

2000; *United States* v. *State of Maryland,* 2004; *United States* v. *Commonwealth of Puerto Rico,* 1997). In one example, the U.S. Department of Justice found that:

> The use of isolation rooms at the facilities is improper and potentially abusive. Staff isolate youth far too frequently and isolation practices are generally outside the requirements of residential treatment or facility security. Due process procedures are significantly lacking and youth are isolated for extended periods of time to suit the staff. One youth was isolated for fifteen days "for acting out and planning an escape." Another youth was isolated for three days for being "sarcastic with a smart mouth." In practice, staff use the isolation rooms to excessively punish youth or simply when the staff are tired of dealing with a specific youth (U.S. Department of Justice, 1995:3).

Parent et al. (1994) found that, although the use of isolation varied considerably among facility types, the rate of shorter isolation (less than 24 hours) was 57 incidents per 100 youth and the rate of longer isolation (more than 24 hours) was 11 incidents per 100 youth.[18] Another national census found that approximately 17 percent of confined youth spend more than 4 hours per month in room confinement (OJJDP, 2002). In addition, an assessment of conditions of confinement in one juvenile detention facility found that approximately 10 percent of confined youth were on disciplinary room confinement status on any given day, often for relatively minor incidents such as horseplay and being disrespectful to staff (John Howard Association, 1998). As a result of subsequent litigation, the facility entered into a consent decree requiring that:

> [R]oom confinement for therapeutic purposes will be employed only upon written order of a . . . qualified mental health professional . . . who has personally observed and examined the resident and has clinically determined that the use of room confinement is necessary to prevent the recipient from causing imminent physical harm to himself or others, and that no other less restrictive intervention is appropriate . . . disciplinary room confinement is used only when no less restrictive form of punishment is appropriate, and that youth who are confined to their rooms are permitted to rejoin the general population when capable of doing so without further disruption to the detention operations (*Jimmy Doe et al.* v. *Cook County et al.,* 2002:23, 34–35).

Data from this national survey of juvenile suicide in confinement appear to show a strong relationship between juvenile suicide and room confinement—62 percent of victims had a history of room confinement before their death and 50 percent of victims were on room confinement status at the time of their death. Perhaps more importantly, 85 percent of victims who died by suicide while on room confinement status died during waking hours (6 a.m. to 9 p.m.).

Although the relationship between suicide and isolation is well documented in the literature on adult inmate suicide (Bonner, 1992; Hayes, 1989), the issue has not been previously explored in depth regarding juvenile suicide. However, Liebling (1993) found that suicidal youth in confinement appeared to feel more isolated, received fewer visits, wrote fewer letters, and missed loved ones more than nonsuicidal youth in custody. Parent et al. (1994) found that 77 percent of confined youth were in facilities that permitted the use of isolation and that rates of suicidal behavior appeared to be higher for youth who were isolated from their peers or assigned to single room housing. Porter (1996) theorized that suicides were more likely to occur in juvenile correctional facilities when youth are further removed from each other, were more alienated, and lacked social integration. Facility officials that promoted these policies were clearly more likely to experience higher rates of suicidal behavior. Similarly, policies and practices that lessened the degree to which confined youth were allowed contact and interaction with one another could increase a facility's risk of experiencing a higher rate of suicidal behavior (Porter, 1996). In conclusion, as one clinician succinctly noted: "When placed in a cold and empty room by themselves, suicidal youth have little to focus on—except all of their reasons for being depressed and the various ways that they can attempt to kill themselves" (Boesky, 2002:210).

Corrective Action

This national survey of juvenile suicide in confinement found that suicide was a seminal event for many facilities. Approximately two-thirds of respondents reported that a mortality review was conducted following the juvenile suicide. In addition, 86.3 percent of these mortality reviews resulted in recommendations to reduce the likelihood of future suicides in the facility. The most frequent recommendations included:

❖ Developing/revising suicide prevention policies (20 cases).

❖ Removing room hazards (20 cases).

❖ Increasing suicide prevention training (18 cases).

❖ Fostering better internal communication among staff and/or external communication with outside agencies (11 cases).

❖ Increasing supervision of youth (10 cases).

❖ Hiring additional direct care staff (9 cases).

❖ Increasing onsite qualified mental health professionals and/or daily assessment of suicidal youth (8 cases).

❖ Providing critical incident stress debriefing to staff and youth (6 cases).

In three cases, facility staff were either disciplined or fired; in two other cases, the facilities were closed.

During the 16-month period from October 1996 through January 1998, one facility sustained five juvenile suicides, three of which occurred during a 2-week period. As a result of the deaths, the facility underwent dramatic changes, including the following:

❖ For several weeks during and after the crisis, lights in all resident rooms were left on 24 hours a day and all youth were observed at 15-minute intervals.

❖ Critical incident stress debriefing was given to all staff and youth.

❖ The number of direct care staff and qualified mental health professionals was dramatically increased.

❖ Basic suicide prevention training was increased to 8-hour instruction, and a 2-hour annual refresher training was developed.

❖ Housing units were renovated to ensure that they provided better staff visibility of youth and were free of obvious protrusions and hazards that might facilitate suicide.

❖ Suicide prevention policies and screening/assessment forms were revised.

In April 1998, an oversight committee of the state legislature met in special session and appropriated approximately $2 million to fund the corrective action measures. Finally, the facility faced and subsequently settled civil litigation arising out of four of the five suicides.

It is not unusual for corrective measures to be implemented following a death or litigation (Hayes, 1994). For example, in March 2003, the Civil Rights Division of the U.S. Department of Justice entered into a settlement agreement with the State of Arkansas regarding conditions of confinement (including two suicides) at one of its juvenile detention facilities. The agreement required several substantive remedial measures, including increased suicide prevention training for staff, better communication among staff in managing suicidal youth, and "revisions in the facility's suicide prevention policy to appropriately clarify what type of staff can place a juvenile on suicide precautions, specify what type of staff can remove a juvenile from such precautions, and provide for sufficient and appropriate daily interactions between qualified mental health personnel and every juvenile on suicide precautions" (*United States* v. *State of Arkansas*, 2003:4). Similar corrective action for juvenile suicide prevention programming has been agreed to through settlement agreements in Arizona (*United States* v. *State of Arizona*, 2004), Georgia (*United States* v. *State of Georgia*, 1998), Kentucky (*United States* v. *Commonwealth of Kentucky*, 1995), Louisiana (*United States* v. *State of Louisiana*, 2000), and Puerto Rico (*United States* v. *Commonwealth of Puerto Rico*, 1997).

Conclusion

Although youth suicide in the community has been identified as a major public health problem, juvenile suicide in confinement has received inadequate attention. The primary goal of this project was to determine the extent and distribution of juvenile suicides in confinement by gathering descriptive data on demographic characteristics of each victim, characteristics of the incident, and characteristics of the juvenile facility that sustained the suicide. In the end, the study compiled significant data on juvenile suicides throughout the country. It is hoped that these findings can be used as a resource for juvenile justice practitioners to expand their knowledge and for juvenile correctional administrators to create and/or revise sound policies and training curriculums on suicide prevention.

Comprehensive Suicide Prevention Programming

Although the study found a significant rate of compliance with individual suicide prevention components, few juvenile facilities that sustained a suicide had all the components of a comprehensive suicide prevention program. Consistent with national correctional standards and practices, all juvenile facilities, regardless of size and type, should have a detailed written suicide prevention policy that addresses each of the following critical components (Council of Juvenile Correctional Administrators, 2003; Hayes, 1999, 2000; National Commission on Correctional Health Care, 1999, 2004; Roush, 1996):

❖ **Training.** All facility, medical, and mental health staff should receive 8 hours of initial suicide prevention training, followed by a minimum of 2 hours of annual refresher training. Training should provide information about predisposing factors, high-risk periods, warning signs and symptoms, identifying suicidal behavior despite the denial of risk, and components of the facility's suicide prevention policy.

❖ **Identification/screening.** Intake screening for suicide risk should take place immediately upon confinement and prior to housing assignment and include inquiry regarding current and past suicidal behavior, earlier mental health treatment, recent significant loss, suicidal behavior by a family member or close friend, suicide risk during prior contact with or confinement in agency, and arresting or transporting officers' opinion whether youth is currently at risk. The policy should include procedures for referral to mental health personnel for further assessment.[19]

❖ **Communication.** At a minimum, facility procedures should enhance communication among facility staff (including medical and mental health personnel) and the arresting/transporting officer(s), family members, and suicidal youth.

❖ **Housing.** Excessive and unjustified isolation should be avoided. Whenever possible, suicidal youth should be housed in the general population, mental health unit, or infirmary, in close proximity to staff. Youth should be housed in suicide-resistant, protrusion-free rooms. Removal of clothing (excluding belts and shoelaces) and use of restraints should be avoided when possible, and should only be used for short periods of time when the youth is engaging in self-destructive behavior.

❖ **Levels of supervision.** Two levels are normally recommended for suicidal youth:

- ◆ Close observation—reserved for youth who are not actively suicidal, but express suicidal ideation and/or have recent histories of self-destructive behavior and are now viewed as potentially suicidal—requires supervision at staggered intervals not to exceed every 15 minutes. In addition, a youth who denies suicidal ideation or does not threaten suicide, but demonstrates other concerning behavior (through actions, current circumstances, or recent history) indicating the potential for self-injury, should be placed on close observation.

- ◆ Constant observation—reserved for youth who are actively suicidal (threatening/engaging in the act)—requires supervision on a continuous, uninterrupted basis.

In addition, an intermediate level of supervision can be used with observation at staggered intervals not to exceed every 5 minutes. Other supervision aides (e.g., closed-circuit television, companions or watchers) can be used as a supplement to, but not as a substitute for, these observation levels.

❖ **Intervention.** A facility's policy regarding intervention should be threefold:

- ◆ All staff should be trained in standard first aid and cardiopulmonary resuscitation (CPR).

- ◆ Any staff member who discovers a youth attempting suicide should immediately respond, survey the scene to ensure the emergency is genuine, alert other staff to call for medical personnel, and begin life-saving measures.

- ◆ Staff should never presume that the youth is dead, but rather initiate and continue appropriate life-saving measures until relieved by medical personnel.

All housing units should contain a first aid kit, pocket mask or mouth shield, Ambu bag, and rescue tool (to quickly cut through fibrous material).

❖ **Reporting.** In the event of an attempted or completed suicide, all appropriate facility officials should be notified through the chain of command. All staff who came in contact with the victim before the incident (or in responding to the incident) should submit a statement as to their full knowledge of the youth and the incident.

❖ **Followup/mortality review.** All staff (and youth) involved in the incident should be offered critical incident stress debriefing. If resources permit, a psychological autopsy is recommended. Every completed suicide and serious suicide attempt (i.e., requiring hospitalization) should be examined by a review process. Ideally, the review should be coordinated by an outside agency or facility to ensure impartiality. The mortality review, separate and apart from other formal investigations that may be required to determine the cause of death, should be multidisciplinary (i.e., involve correctional, mental health, and medical personnel) and include a critical inquiry of the following:

- ◆ The circumstances surrounding the incident.

- ◆ Facility procedures relevant to the incident.

- ◆ All relevant training received by involved staff.

- ◆ Pertinent medical and mental health services/reports involving the victim.

- ◆ Possible precipitating factors leading to the suicide.

- ◆ Recommendations, if any, for changes in policy, training, physical plant, medical or mental health services, and operational procedures.

Staff Training

Although findings from this study suggest that some type of suicide prevention training was conducted in most facilities, only one-third of facilities experiencing a suicide provided annual training and very few facilities provided a full day of training to their personnel. On the basis of this information, coupled with recent census data indicating that almost a quarter of all intake screening for suicide risk in juvenile facilities throughout the country is conducted by untrained personnel (OJJDP, 2002), administrators would be prudent to ensure that all direct care, medical, and mental health personnel receive both pre-service and annual instruction in suicide prevention.

Further, for the most part, current suicide prevention training curriculums used in juvenile facilities throughout the country rely on information gathered about adult inmate suicide and youth suicide in the community. Findings from this study demonstrate that several differences exist between adult inmate suicide and suicides in juvenile facilities, including confinement status, intoxication, length of confinement before suicide, and time of day. These significant differences should discourage using training curriculums from the adult correctional field in the prevention of suicide in juvenile facilities. Although suicide prevention in all types of correctional facilities has common ground, the differences between juvenile and adult inmate suicides warrant development within juvenile facilities of separate training curriculums targeted to suicide prevention.

Basic suicide prevention training for direct care, medical, and mental health personnel who work in juvenile facilities should include discussion of the following issues: why facility environments are conducive to suicidal behavior, staff attitudes about suicide, potential predisposing factors to suicide, warning signs and symptoms, identification of suicide risk despite the youth's denial, high-risk periods, components of the facility's suicide prevention policy, instruction regarding the proper role of staff in responding to a suicide attempt (including a mock drill), critical incident stress debriefing, liability issues, and recent serious suicide attempts and/or suicides within the facility/agency.

Staff are at a distinct disadvantage in the identification and management of suicidal youth if they have not been adequately trained in suicide prevention.

Detention Centers

Findings from this study indicate that a significant percentage of unknown responses to survey questions relating to several personal characteristics of the victim (including histories of substance abuse, medical problems, emotional abuse, physical abuse, sexual abuse, and mental illness) came from detention centers.[20] In addition, suicide victims housed in detention centers had a lower percentage of reported histories of suicidal behavior, perhaps suggesting that these facilities fail to inquire about such history. Finally, although the study found that many facility types lacked comprehensive suicide prevention programming at time of suicide, detention centers had the lowest percentage (approximately 10 percent).

According to the National Juvenile Detention Association (NJDA), juvenile detention is defined as "the temporary and safe custody of juveniles who are accused of conduct subject to the jurisdiction of the court who require a restricted environment for their own and the community's protection while pending legal action" (National Juvenile Detention Association, 1990:1). The findings from this study support NJDA's position that youth with severe mental illness should be provided services in "the appropriate therapeutic environment . . . when juvenile detention facilities are forced to house youth with severe mental health issues, NJDA promotes the provision of adequate services by appropriately trained and licensed specialists" (National Juvenile Detention Association, 2001). Deficiencies in intake screening and overall suicide prevention programming within detention centers experiencing suicides warrant immediate attention to ensure the provision of basic, yet comprehensive, suicide prevention programming.

Data Limitations

Given the epidemiological data regarding youth suicide in the community, coupled with the increased risk factors associated with confined youth, the reported number of suicides in this study would appear low. However, this study identified more deaths per year than a contemporary national census of juvenile facilities (OJJDP, 2002), and many experts believe that the current "self-reporting" of juvenile suicides in custody is underreported (Sullivan, 1995; Twedt, 2001b). Despite concerted efforts by project staff to locate all possible juvenile suicides during the 5-year study period, whether every death was identified remains uncertain.

Approximately 13 percent of the reported suicides in this study were identified through nontraditional sources (including newspaper articles and the project director's consultation with facilities sustaining the deaths). In addition, more than one-third of the reported suicides were unknown to any state agency (e.g., departments of juvenile corrections or agencies responsible for licensing and regulatory services). Most of the deaths that were unknown to state agencies occurred in either county detention centers or private residential treatment centers.[21] Many of the reported suicides in this study were also unknown to many child advocacy agencies.

Research

The problem of juvenile suicides in confinement would benefit from further research. For example, possible precipitating factors to the suicides reported in this study were identified in only slightly more than one-third of the cases. This indicates either uncertainty of the term, inadequate review of the circumstances surrounding the death, limited knowledge of the victim's background, or all of the above. Regardless of the reasons, further inquiry of possible precipitating factors of juvenile suicide is critically important to increasing understanding of the problem.

Although approximately half the victims in this study were under room confinement at the time of their death, further research is necessary to explore the relationship between suicide and isolation. Despite the fact that youth were alone in their rooms between the hours of midnight and 6 a.m., with ample opportunity and privacy to engage in self-injurious behavior, few suicides took place during this 6-hour period. Instead, approximately half of all deaths occurred during a 6-hour period between 6 p.m. and midnight—almost a third occurred between 6 p.m. and 9 p.m. Perhaps most important, the majority of victims who committed suicide while on room confinement status died during waking hours. These are periods in which youth are normally either involved in programming or back on their housing units, interacting with staff and peers—perhaps more likely to become involved in confrontations and/or behavior that results in room confinement. Further research is needed to explore this issue.

Finally, although only a small percentage of victims committed suicide following more than 12 months of custody, the average length of confinement before suicide for these youth was quite high (i.e., approximately 22 months), suggesting that prolonged confinement might have been one of the precipitating factors in the suicides. This issue is also worthy of further study.

Challenges

Findings from this study pose formidable challenges for juvenile correctional and healthcare officials and their staffs. For example, although room confinement remains a staple in most juvenile facilities, its use needs to be carefully scrutinized. In addition, as data show that suicides can occur at any time during a youth's stay in a facility a continuum of comprehensive suicide prevention services aimed at the collaborative identification, continued assessment, and safe management of youth at risk for self-harm, is required to address the problem effectively.

Notes

1. The only national survey on the incidence of juvenile suicides in custody contained several flaws in the calculation of suicide rates (Flaherty, 1980). Reanalysis of suicide rates in that survey found youth suicide in juvenile detention centers to be more than four times greater than in the general population (Memory, 1989).

2. Duclos et al. (1998) also found high rates of psychiatric disorders among Native American youth confined in juvenile facilities.

3. The reporting period was October 1, 1999, to September 30, 2000.

4. The National Center for Health Statistics, Centers for Disease Control, which collects annual vital statistics mortality data, does not separate out data between the community and custodial institutions, nor does it collect data on the circumstances, characteristics, and precipitating causes of suicide. In addition, although the Deaths in Custody Reporting Act of 2000 became Public Law No. 106–297 on October 13, 2000, the collected data is cursory, gathered on a voluntary basis, and is limited to the cause, date, time, and place of death and age, sex, race, and legal status of the victim.

5. The National Center on Institutions and Alternatives was assisted on the project by two prominent national juvenile justice organizations (the National Juvenile Detention Association and the Council of Juvenile Correctional Administrators) and a consultant team composed of four prominent juvenile justice practitioners and researchers (G. David Curry, Ph.D., Robert E. DeComo, Ph.D., Barbara C. Dooley, Ph.D., and David W. Roush, Ph.D.). In addition, Cedrick Heraux, a doctoral student at Michigan State University, provided both data entry and data analysis support to the project.

6. Facilities were identified through OJJDP's Census of Juveniles in Residential Placement (1999). A small percentage of facilities were either closed or could not be located, and thus presumed to be closed.

7. To encourage a high rate of response, the cover letter was co-signed by officials of both the National Juvenile Detention Association and the Council of Juvenile Correctional Administrators, and business reply envelopes were enclosed with the survey instruments.

8. By definition, detention centers hold juveniles for short terms in a physically restrictive environment pending juvenile court action, or following adjudication pending disposition, placement, or transfer. Reception centers are short-term facilities that hold juveniles committed by courts and that do screening and assessment to assign them to appropriate facilities. Training schools are long-term facilities in which treatment and programming are provided in an environment with strict physical and staff controls. Ranches, camps, and farms are long-term residential facilities that do not require the strict confinement of a training school, often allowing offenders greater contact with the community. This last category includes "residential treatment center" and "boot camp."

9. During this followup process, the project director was assisted by staff of the Council of Juvenile Correctional Administrators.

10. For comparative purposes, data collected from OJJDP's Census of Juveniles in Residential Placement was limited to the following: gender, age, race, placement authority, most serious offense charged, and adjudication status.

11. For purposes of this study, offenses were broken down into six categories: property offenses included burglary, grand larceny, petty larceny, auto theft, robbery (other), receiving stolen property, shoplifting, arson, breaking and entering, entering without breaking, counterfeiting, forgery, embezzlement, vandalism, and carrying a concealed weapon; person offenses included murder, negligent manslaughter, armed robbery, rape, indecent assault, assault, battery, sexual assault, aggravated assault, and kidnapping; status offenses included running away, truancy, incorrigibility, curfew violation, and loitering; probation violation offenses included any technical violation of the terms of probation and/or parole; public order offenses included alcohol-related charges (intoxication, liquor law violation, driving under the influence), resisting arrest, disorderly conduct, prostitution, sex offenses (other), vagrancy, unauthorized use of a motor vehicle, and minor traffic offenses; and drug offenses included possession, use, and distribution of any controlled dangerous substance or narcotic.

12. However, the average length of confinement for the 10 victims who committed suicide after more than 12 months in custody was 21.8 months.

13. For comparative purposes, although lengths of stay within juvenile facilities throughout the country vary considerably, earlier OJJDP research has shown the average length of stay in the four facility types to be as follows: detention center (15 days), training school/secure facility (7.5 months), reception/diagnostic center (34 days), and residential treatment center (6.5 months) (see Parent, Leiter, Kennedy, Livens, Wentworth and Wilcox, 1994).

14. For the most part, survey respondents did not report the victims' mental illness according to *Diagnostic and Statistical Manual (DSM) III* or *IV* editions.

15. The circumstances that led to room confinement included failure to follow program rules or inappropriate behavior (47.3 percent), threat of or actual physical abuse of staff or peers (42.1 percent), and other (10.6 percent), which included two cases of standard procedure for new intake, one case of court-ordered confinement, and one case of group confinement during a shift change.

16. In 1995, OJJDP contracted with the Council of Juvenile Correctional Administrators to develop, field test, and implement performance-based standards for juvenile correctional and detention facilities. The Performance-based Standards Project offers a systematic method for facilities to measure outcomes and provides guidance for facilities to review their practices and to take corrective action.

17. This finding is somewhat consistent with an earlier OJJDP research finding that approximately 72 percent of juveniles are housed in facilities with 250 or fewer beds, although only 21 percent are housed in facilities with 50 or fewer beds (see Parent et al., 1994).

18. Parent et al. (1994) could not calculate the incidence of "time-out" or other forms of room confinement that occurred for durations of less than 1 hour because its use was frequently not documented.

19. Several intake screening and assessment forms are available for the identification of suicide risk, including the "Intake Screening Form/Suicide Risk Assessment" (Hayes, 1999), the recently developed "Juvenile Suicide Assessment" (Galloucis and Francek, 2002), and the Massachusetts Youth Screening Instrument-MAYSI-2 (Grisso and Barnum, 2000).

20. Communication among agencies also appeared to be a problem in several cases. Surveys were received from several detention centers in which respondents complained that they had been temporarily "holding" the victim for another jurisdiction (e.g., state correctional facility, probation office) and knew little, if anything, about the youth. As one facility director stated, "I do not know the answers to some of these questions because the child was not from our county. He was being housed here in a state-contract bed."

21. Although the study found that 27 percent of the total number of suicides (N=110) occurred in private facilities, many of which were residential treatment centers, approximately two-thirds (67 percent) of private facilities did not respond to survey requests.

References

Alessi, N., McManus, M., Brickman, A., and Grapentine, L. 1984. Suicidal behavior among serious juvenile offenders. *American Journal of Psychiatry* 141(2):286–287.

American Correctional Association. 1991. *Standards for Juvenile Detention Facilities and Standards for Juvenile Correctional Facilities.* Laurel, MD: American Correctional Association.

American Psychiatric Association. 2000. *Diagnostic and Statistical Manual of Mental Disorders (DSM-IV-TR).* Washington, DC: American Psychiatric Association.

Amnesty International. 1998. *Betraying the Young: Human Rights Violations Against Children in the U.S. Justice System.* New York, NY: Amnesty International.

Anno, B. 1984. The availability of health services for juvenile offenders: Preliminary results of a national survey. *Journal of Prison and Jail Health* 4(2):77–90.

Arias, E., Anderson, R., Kung, H., Murphy, S., and Kochanek, K. 2003. Deaths: Final data for 2001. *National Vital Statistics Report 52(3).* Hyattsville, MD: National Center for Health Statistics.

Austin, J., Krisberg, B., DeComo, R., Rudenstine, S., and Del Rosario, D. 1995. *Juveniles Taken Into Custody: Fiscal Year 1993 Report.* Washington, DC: U.S. Department of Justice, Office of Justice Programs, Office of Juvenile Justice and Delinquency Prevention.

Boesky, L. 2002. *Juvenile Offenders With Mental Health Disorders: Who Are They and What Do We Do With Them?* Lanham, MD: American Correctional Association.

Bonner, R. 1992. Isolation, seclusion, and psychological vulnerability as risk factors for suicide behind bars. In *Assessment and Prediction of Suicide,* edited by R. Maris et al. New York, NY: Guilford Press, pp. 398–419.

Brent, D. 1995. Risk factors for adolescent suicide and suicidal behavior: Mental and substance abuse disorders, family environmental factors, and life stress. *Suicide and Life Threatening Behavior* 25(Supplement):52–63.

Bureau of Justice Statistics. 2005 (August). *Suicide and Homicide in State Prisons and Local Jails.* Washington, DC: U.S. Department of Justice, Office of Justice Programs, Bureau of Justice Statistics.

Burrell, S. 1999. *Improving Conditions of Confinement in Secure Detention Centers.* Baltimore, MD: Annie E. Casey Foundation.

Carmona, R.H. 2005. *Suicide Prevention Among Native American Youth.* Prepared Remarks of Richard H. Carmona, M.D., M.P.H., F.A.C.S., Surgeon General, U.S. Public Health Service, U.S. Department of Health and Human Services. Testimony Before the Indian Affairs Committee, U.S. Senate, June 15, 2005.

Chapman, J., Wasilesky, S., and Zuccaro, M. 2000. Assessment of the psychiatric needs of children in Connecticut's juvenile detention centers. Unpublished report. Rocky Hill, CT: State of Connecticut, Judicial Branch-Court Support Services Division.

Chowanec, G., Josephson, A., Coleman, C., and Davis, H. 1991. Self-harming behavior in incarcerated male delinquent adolescents. *Journal of the American Academy of Child and Adolescent Psychiatry* 30(2):202–207.

Coalition for Juvenile Justice. 1999. *Ain't No Place Anybody Would Want To Be: Conditions of Confinement for Youth.* Washington, DC: Coalition for Juvenile Justice.

Coalition for Juvenile Justice. 2000. *Handle With Care: Serving the Mental Health Needs of Young Offenders.* Washington, DC: Coalition for Juvenile Justice.

Cocozza, J., and Skowyra, K. 2000. Youth with mental health disorders: Issues and emerging responses. *Juvenile Justice* 7(1):3–13.

Council of Juvenile Correctional Administrators. 2003. *Performance-based Standards (PbS) for Youth Correction and Detention Facilities: PbS Goals, Standards, Outcome Measures, Expected Practices and Processes.* Braintree, MA: Council of Juvenile Correctional Administrators.

Davis, D., Bean, G., Schumacher, J., and Stringer, T. 1991. Prevalence of emotional disorders in a juvenile justice institutional population. *American Journal of Forensic Psychology* 9:1–13.

DeComo, R., Tunis, S., Krisberg, B., Herrera, N., Rudenstine, S., and Del Rosario, D. 1995. *Juveniles Taken Into Custody: Fiscal Year 1992.* Washington, DC: U.S. Department of Justice, Office of Justice Programs, Office of Juvenile Justice and Delinquency Prevention.

Dembo, R., Williams, L., Wish, E., Berry, E., Getreu, A., Washburn, M., and Schmeidler, J. 1990. Examination of the relationships among drug use, emotional/psychological problems, and crime among youths entering a juvenile detention center. *The International Journal of the Addictions* 25:1301–1340.

Domalanta, D., Risser, W., Roberts, R., and Risser, J. 2003. Prevalence of depression and other psychiatric disorders among incarcerated youths. *Journal of the American Academy of Child and Adolescent Psychiatry* 42(4):477–484.

Duclos, C., Beals, J., Novins, D., Martin, C., Jewett, C., and Manson, S. 1998. Prevalence of common psychiatric disorders among American Indian adolescent detainees. *Journal of the American Academy of Child and Adolescent Psychiatry* 37(8):866–873.

Duclos, C., LeBeau, W., and Elias, G. 1994. American Indian suicidal behavior in detention environments: Cause for continued basic and applied research. *Jail Suicide Update* 5(4):4–9.

Edens, J., and Otto, R. 1997. Prevalence of mental disorders among youth in the juvenile justice system. *Focal Point* (Spring):1–8.

Esposito, C., and Clum, G. 2002. Social support and problem-solving as moderators of the relationship between childhood abuse and suicidality: Applications to a delinquent population. *Journal of Traumatic Stress* 15(2):137–146.

Flaherty, M. 1980. *An Assessment of the National Incidence of Juvenile Suicide in Adult Jails, Lockups, and Juvenile Detention Centers.* Champaign, IL: University of Illinois.

Galloucis, M., and Francek, H. 2002. The juvenile suicide assessment: An instrument for the assessment and management of suicide risk with incarcerated juveniles. *International Journal of Emergency Mental Health* 4(3):181–199.

Goldstrom, I., Jaiquan, F., Henderson, M., Male, A., and Manderscheid, R. 2001. The availability of mental health services to young people in juvenile justice facilities: A national survey. In *Mental Health, United States, 2000.* Washington, DC: U.S. Department of Health and Human Services, Substance Abuse and Mental Health Services Administration, pp. 248–268.

Grisso, T., and Barnum, R. 2000. *The Massachusetts Youth Screening Instrument-2: User's Manual and Technical Report.* Worcester, MA: University of Massachusetts Medical Center.

Hayes, L. 1989. National study of jail suicides: Seven years later. *Psychiatric Quarterly* 60(1):7–29.

Hayes, L. 1994. Juvenile suicide in confinement: An overview and summary of one system's approach. *Juvenile and Family Court Journal* 45(2):65–75.

Hayes, L. 1995. Prison suicide: An overview and a guide to prevention. *The Prison Journal* 75(4):431–455.

Hayes, L. 1999. *Suicide Prevention in Juvenile Correction and Detention Facilities: A Resource Guide.* South Easton, MA: Council of Juvenile Correctional Administrators.

Hayes, L. 2000. Suicide prevention in juvenile facilities. *Juvenile Justice* 7(1):24–32.

He, X., Felthous, A., Holzer, C., Nathan, P., and Veasey, S. 2001. Factors in prison suicide: One year study in Texas. *Journal of Forensic Sciences* 46(4):896–901.

Jimmy Doe et al. v. Cook County et al. 2002. United States District Court for the Northern District of Illinois, Eastern Division, Civil No. 99-C-3945, Memorandum of Agreement, October.

John Howard Association. 1998. *Assessment of Conditions at the Cook County Juvenile Temporary Detention Center.* Chicago, IL: John Howard Association.

Kempton, T., and Forehand, R. 1992. Suicide attempts among juvenile delinquents: The contribution of mental health factors. *Behaviour Research and Therapy* 30(5):537–541.

Krisberg, B., DeComo, R., Herrera, N., Steketee, M., and Roberts, S. 1991. *Juveniles Taken Into Custody: Fiscal Year 1990 Report.* Washington, DC: U.S. Department of Justice, Office of Justice Programs, Office of Juvenile Justice and Delinquency Prevention.

Liebling, A. 1993. Suicides in young prisoners: A summary. *Death Studies* 17:381– 409.

Mace, D., Rohde, P., and Gnau, V. 1997. Psychological patterns of depression and suicidal behavior of adolescents in a juvenile detention facility. *Journal for Juvenile Justice and Detention Services* 12(1):18–23.

Marsteller, F., Brogan, D., Smith I., Ash, P., Daniels, D., Rolka, D., and Falek, A. 1997. *The Prevalence of Substance Abuse Disorders Among Juveniles Admitted to Regional Youth Detention Centers Operated by the Georgia Department of Children and Youth Services.* Atlanta, GA: CSAT Final Report.

McGarvey, E., Kryzhanovskaya, L., Koopman, C., Waite, D., and Canterbury, R. 1999. Incarcerated adolescents' distress and suicidality in relation to parental bonding styles. *Crisis* 20(4):164–170.

McGarvey, E., and Waite, D. 2000. *Mental Health Needs Among Juveniles Committed to the Virginia Department of Juvenile Justice.* Juvenile Justice Fact Sheet. Charlottesville, VA: University of Virginia, Institute of Law, Psychiatry and Public Policy.

Memory, J. 1989. Juvenile suicides in secure detention facilities: Correction of published rates. *Death Studies* 13:455–463.

Mitchell, J., and Varley, C. 1990. Isolation and restraint in juvenile correctional facilities. *Journal of the American Academy of Child and Adolescent Psychiatry* 29(2):251–255.

Morris, R., Harrison, E., Knox, G., Tromanhauser, E., Marquis, D., and Watts, L.L. 1995. Health Risk Behavioral Survey from 39 juvenile correctional facilities in the United States. *Journal of Adolescent Health* 17(6):334–344.

National Commission on Correctional Health Care. 1995. *Standards for Health Services in Juvenile Detention and Confinement Facilities.* Chicago, IL: National Commission on Correctional Health Care.

National Commission on Correctional Health Care. 1999. *Standards for Health Services in Juvenile Detention and Confinement Facilities.* Chicago, IL: National Commission on Correctional Health Care.

National Commission on Correctional Health Care. 2004. *Standards for Health Services in Juvenile Detention and Confinement Facilities.* Chicago, IL: National Commission on Correctional Health Care.

National Juvenile Detention Association. 1990. *Position Statement: Definition of Juvenile Detention.* Richmond, KY: National Juvenile Detention Association.

National Juvenile Detention Association. 2001. *Position Statement: Use of Juvenile Detention Facilities for Youth With Severe Mental Health Issues.* Richmond, KY: National Juvenile Detention Association.

Office of Juvenile Justice and Delinquency Prevention. 1999. *Census of Juveniles in Residential Placement.* Washington, DC: U.S. Department of Justice, Office of Justice Programs, Office of Juvenile Justice and Delinquency Prevention.

Office of Juvenile Justice and Delinquency Prevention. 2002. *2000 Juvenile Residential Facility Census.* Unpublished data. Washington, DC: U.S. Department of Justice, Office of Justice Programs, Office of Juvenile Justice and Delinquency Prevention.

Otto, R., Greenstein, J., Johnson, M., and Friedman, R. 1992. Prevalence of mental disorders among youth in the juvenile justice system. In *Responding to the Mental Health Needs of Youth in the Juvenile Justice System.* Seattle, WA: National Coalition for the Mentally Ill in the Criminal Justice System, pp. 7–48.

Parent, D., Leiter, V., Kennedy, S., Livens, L., Wentworth, D., and Wilcox, S. 1994. *Conditions of Confinement: Juvenile Detention and Corrections Facilities.* Washington, DC: U.S. Department of Justice, Office of Justice Programs, Office of Juvenile Justice and Delinquency Prevention.

Penn, J., Esposito, C., Schaeffer, L., Fritz, G., and Spirito, A. 2003. Suicide attempts and self-mutilative behavior in a juvenile correctional facility. *Journal of the American Academy of Child and Adolescent Psychiatry* 42(7):762–769.

Porter, C. 1996. Suicide among juvenile offenders: The impact of social integration on suicidal behaviors in juvenile confinement facilities. Unpublished master's thesis, Michigan State University.

Puritz, P., and Scali, M. 1998. *Beyond the Walls: Improving Conditions of Confinement for Youth in Custody.* Washington, DC: U.S. Department of Justice, Office of Justice Programs, Office of Juvenile Justice and Delinquency Prevention.

Robertson, A., and Husain, J. 2001. *Prevalence of Mental illness and Substance Abuse Disorders Among Incarcerated Juvenile Offenders.* Jackson, MS: Mississippi Department of Public Safety and Mississippi Department of Mental Health.

Rohde, P., Seeley, J., and Mace, D. 1997. Correlates of suicidal behavior in a juvenile detention population. *Suicide and Life-Threatening Behavior* 27(2):164–175.

Rosenbaum, S. 1999. Civil rights issues in juvenile detention and correctional systems. *Corrections Today* (October):148–156.

Roush, D. 1996. *Desktop Guide to Good Juvenile Detention Practice.* Washington, DC: U.S. Department of Justice, Office of Justice Programs, Office of Juvenile Justice and Delinquency Prevention.

Sanislow, C., Grilo, C., Fehon, D., Axelrod, S., and McGlashan, T. 2003. Correlates of suicide risk in juvenile detainees and adolescent in-patients. *Journal of the American Academy of Child and Adolescent Psychiatry* 42(2):234–240.

Shelton, D. 2000. Health Status of Young Offenders and Their Families. *Journal of Nursing Scholarship* 32(2):173–178.

Sickmund, M., and Wan, T. 2001. *Census of Juveniles in Residential Placement Databook.* Washington, DC: U.S. Department of Justice, Office of Justice Programs, Office of Juvenile Justice and Delinquency Prevention.

Steiner, H., Garcia, I., and Matthews, Z. 1997. Posttraumatic stress disorder in incarcerated juvenile delinquents. *Journal of the American Academy of Child and Adolescent Psychiatry* 36(3):357–365.

Substance Abuse and Mental Health Services Administration. 2001. *Summary of Findings From the 2000 National Household Survey on Drug Abuse.* NHSDA Series: H-13, DHHS Publication No. SMA 01-3549. Rockville, MD: U.S. Department of Health and Human Services, Substance Abuse and Mental Health Services Administration.

Sullivan, C. 1995. Juvenile custody suicides blamed on apathy, impulse, gaps in care. *Los Angeles Times* (March 12):A1,18.

Teplin, L., Abram, K., McClelland, G., Dulcan, M., and Mericle, A. 2002. Psychiatric disorders in youth in juvenile detention. *Archives in General Psychiatry* 59:1133–1143.

Trupin, E., and Patterson, R. 2003. *Report of Findings of Mental Health and Substance Abuse Treatment Services to Youth in California Youth Authority Facilities,* December.

Twedt, S. 2001a. Juvenile lockups ill-equipped to care for young people considering suicide. *Pittsburgh Post-Gazette* (December 9):1.

Twedt, S. 2001b. Lack of options keeps mentally disturbed youth locked up. *Pittsburgh Post-Gazette* (July 15):1.

Underwood, L., and Berenson, D. 2001. *Mental Health Programming in Youth Correction and Detention Facilities: A Resource Guide.* South Easton, MA: Council of Juvenile Correctional Administrators.

United States v. *Commonwealth of Kentucky.* 1995. United States District Court for the Western District of Kentucky, *Consent Decree,* December 4.

United States v. *Commonwealth of Puerto Rico.* 1997. Civil No. 94-2080 (CC), United States District Court for the District of Puerto Rico, *Remedial Provision of Settlement Agreement,* October 7.

United States v. *State of Arizona.* 2004. *CRIPA Investigation of Adobe Mountain School and Black Canyon School in Phoenix, Arizona, and Catalina Mountain School in Tucson, Arizona,* January 23.

United States v. *State of Arkansas.* 2003. United States District Court for the Eastern District of Arkansas, Court-Entered Settlement, March 10.

United States v. *State of Georgia.* 1998. United States District Court for the Northern District of Georgia, Memorandum of Agreement Between the United States and the State of Georgia Concerning Georgia Juvenile Justice Facilities, March 18.

United States v. *State of Louisiana.* 2000. Civil No. 98-947-B-1, United States District Court for the Middle District of Louisiana, Memorandum in Support of the United States' Motion for a Preliminary Injunction Regarding Conditions of Confinement at the Jena Juvenile Justice Center, March 30.

United States v. *State of Maryland.* 2004. *Investigation of Cheltenham Youth Facility in Cheltenham, Maryland, and the Charles H. Hickey, Jr. School in Baltimore, Maryland,* April 9.

U.S. Department of Health and Human Services. 1999. *The Surgeon General's Call To Action To Prevent Suicide, 1999.* Washington, DC: U.S. Department of Health and Human Services.

U.S. Department of Justice, Civil Rights Division, Special Litigation Section. 1995. *Notice of Findings of Investigation of Various Kentucky Treatment Centers, July 28, 1995.* Washington, DC: U.S. Department of Justice, Civil Rights Division, Special Litigation Section.

U.S. Department of Justice, Civil Rights Division, Special Litigation Section. 2003. *CRIPA Investigation of Oakley and Columbia Training Schools in Raymond and Columbia, Mississippi, June 19, 2003.* Washington, DC: U.S. Department of Justice, Civil Rights Division, Special Litigation Section.

U.S. House of Representatives. 2004. *Incarceration of Youth Who Are Waiting for Community Mental Health Services in the United States.* Washington, DC: U.S. House of Representatives, Committee on Government Reform (Minority Staff), Special Investigations Division, July.

White, T., and Schimmel, D. 1995. Suicide prevention in federal prisons: A successful five-step program. In *Prison Suicide: An Overview and Guide to Prevention,* edited by L. Hayes. Washington, DC: U.S. Department of Justice, National Institute of Corrections, pp. 46–57.

Woolf, A., and Funk, S. 1985. Epidemiology of trauma in a population of incarcerated youth. *Pediatrics* 75(3):463–468.

Appendix A: Phase 1 Survey Instrument

JUVENILE SUICIDE IN CONFINEMENT: A NATIONAL SURVEY
PHASE 1

NATIONAL CENTER ON INSTITUTIONS AND ALTERNATIVES
Acting as Collecting Agency for the
OFFICE OF JUVENILE JUSTICE AND DELINQUENCY PREVENTION
U.S. DEPARTMENT OF JUSTICE

Dear Facility Director:

On behalf of the Office of Justice and Delinquency Prevention, U.S. Department of Justice, the National Center on Institutions and Alternatives is conducting the first national survey of juvenile suicide in confinement. The goal of this two-phase project, which is being conducted with the full support and assistance of both the National Juvenile Detention Association and Council of Juvenile Correctional Administrators, will be to gather descriptive data on demographic characteristics of suicide victims, characteristics of the incident, and characteristics of the facility sustaining the suicide. A report of the findings will be available as a resource tool for both juvenile justice practitioners in expanding their knowledge base, and juvenile correctional administrators in creating and/or revising policies and training curricula on suicide prevention.

During Phase 1, we are sending this survey to all public and private juvenile detention centers/homes, training schools/secure facilities, receptions diagnostic centers, residential treatment centers, and ranches, camps and farms in the country. *On the reverse side of this form, we are asking whether your current or former facility had a suicide and/or critical suicide attempt during the five-year period of January 1, 1995 through December 31, 1999.*

We ask that you complete and return this form within 30 days *only* if your current or former facility sustained a suicide and/or critical suicide attempt during this time period. A self-addressed, business reply envelope is enclosed for your convenience.

PARTICIPATION IN THIS SURVEY PROCESS IS VOLUNTARY. DATA PROVIDED WILL BE CODED AND HELD IN THE STRICTEST CONFIDENCE. RESULTS OF THIS STUDY WILL BE PRESENTED IN SUMMARY FASHION, THEREFORE, VICTIM AND FACILITY NAMES WILL *NOT* APPEAR IN ANY PROJECT REPORT.

Should you have any questions or concerns regarding completion of this form or our study, please contact Lindsay M. Hayes, Project Director, National Center on Institutions and Alternatives (NCIA), 40 Lantern Lane, Mansfield, Massachusetts 02048, 508/337-8806, e-mail: Lhayesta@aol.com, or 508/337-3083 (fax).

Your cooperation and support of this project are greatly appreciated.

Sincerely,

Lindsay M. Hayes, Project Director
National Center on Institutions and Alternatives

Edward J. Loughran, Executive Director
Council of Juvenile Correctional Administrators

Earl L. Dunlap, Executive Director
National Juvenile Detention Association

DEFINITIONS

SUICIDE: Any death of a youth from a self-inflicted act. *(Note: for purposes of this study, a youth who attempts suicide in the facility yet later dies enroute to, or at, a hospital or other health care provider, is classified as a "juvenile facility suicide" and should be reported below.)*

CRITICAL SUICIDE ATTEMPT: Any self-inflicted act by a youth that results in transport our of the facility to a hospital or other health care provider for medical attention and hospitalization.

DETENTION CENTER/HOME: A short-term facility that provides custody in a physically restricting environment pending adjudication or, following, adjudication, pending disposition, placement, or transfer.

TRAINING SCHOOL/SECURE FACILITY: A long-term facility for adjudicated youth typically under strict physical/staff controls.

RECEPTION/DIAGNOSTIC CENTER: A short-term facility that screens youth committed by courts and assigns them to appropriate facilities.

RANCH, CAMP, or FARM: A long-term residential facility for youth whose behavior does not require the strict confinement of a training school, often allowing them greater contact with the community. Includes "residential treatment facility" and "boot camp."

PUBLIC FACILITY: A facility under the direct administrative and operational control of a state or local government.

PRIVATE FACILITY: A facility (either profit or non-profit making) subject to government licensing but under the direct administrative and operational control of a private enterprise. May include facilities that include public and private funding.

RESIDENT: Any youth, either classified as a delinquent, status offender, or non-offender (dependent, neglected, abused, etc.) that resides in a public or private facility.

QUESTIONS

Please indicate below the total number of SUICIDES and/or CRITICAL SUICIDE ATTEMPTS that occurred in your current/former facility during the five-year period of January 1, 1995 through December 31, 1999. complete this form only if your facility had a suicide(s) and/or critical suicide attempt(s) during this time period.

1. Our facility had the following incidents by residents:

_____ SUIDCIDE(S) and/or _____ CRITICAL SUICIDE ATTEMPT(S) in **1995**
_____ SUIDCIDE(S) and/or _____ CRITICAL SUICIDE ATTEMPT(S) in **1996**
_____ SUIDCIDE(S) and/or _____ CRITICAL SUICIDE ATTEMPT(S) in **1997**
_____ SUIDCIDE(S) and/or _____ CRITICAL SUICIDE ATTEMPT(S) in **1998**
_____ SUIDCIDE(S) and/or _____ CRITICAL SUICIDE ATTEMPT(S) in **1999**

2. Our facility is _____ PUBLIC _____ PRIVATE

3. Our facility is best described as a:

_____ DETENTION CENTER/HOME
_____ TRAINING SCHOOL/SECURE FACILITY
_____ RECEPTION/DIOAGNOSTIC CENTER
_____ RANCH, CAMP, or FARM
_____ OTHER (Explain): _____

THE FOLLOWING WILL BE USED FOR INTERNAL PURPOSES ONLY:

4. Completed by (name/title): _____

5. Name of Facility: _____

6. Address: _____

City: _____ State: _____ Zip code: _____

7. Telephone: _____

8. Date Completed: _____

**PLEASE RETURN THIS COMPLETED FOR IN THE ENCLOSED
BUSINESS REPLY ENVELOPE WITHIN 30 DAYS TO:
NCIA ● 40 Lantern Lane ● Mansfield, MA 02048
or Fax to 508/337-3083**

Appendix B: Phase 2 Survey Instrument

PHASE 2
JUVENILE SUICIDE IN CONFINEMENT: A NATIONAL SURVEY
NATIONAL CENTER ON INSTITUTIONS AND ALTERNATIVES
Acting as Collecting Agency for the
OFFICE OF JUVENILE JUSTICE AND DELINQUENCY PREVENTION
U.S. DEPARTMENT OF JUSTICE

Items contained in this questionnaire refer to a suicide that occurred in your facility between January 1, 1995 and December 31, 1999 as identified during Phase 1 of the Juvenile Suicide in Confinement study. Please complete the following questionnaire by checking the appropriate boxes and/or filling in the blanks. Definitions for certain terms used in this questionnaire appear on page 7.

DATA PROVIDED WILL BE CODED AND HELD IN THE STRICTEST CONFIDENCE. RESULTS OF THIS STUDY WILL BE PRESENTED IN SUMMARY FASHION, THEREFORE, VICTIM AND FACILITY NAMES WILL *NOT* APPEAR IN ANY PROJECT REPORT.

We ask that you complete and return this questionnaire within 30 days. A self-addressed, business reply envelope is enclosed for your convenience. Should you have any questions or concerns regarding completion of this questionnaire, please contact Lindsay M. Hayes, Project Director, National Center on Institutions and Alternatives (NCIA), 40 Lantern Lane, Mansfield, Massachusetts 02048, 508/337-8806, e-mail: Lhayesta@aol.com, or 508/337-3083 (fax).

NAME OF FACILITY _____ STATE _____

PART A: PERSONAL CHARACTERISTICS OF VICTIM

1) Victim's Name (or any other identifiable notation):

_____

Last	First	Middle

2) Race/Ethnicity:
   (1) _____ Caucasian   (4) _____ American Indian
   (2) _____ African-American   (8) _____ Other (Specify _____)
   (3) _____ Hispanic   (9) _____ Unknown

3) Sex:
   (1) _____ Male   (2) _____ Female

4) Date-of-Birth: ___/___/___   or   _____ Years-Old

5) Living Status:
   (1) _____ Self   (5) _____ Foster Parent/Guardian
   (2) _____ One Parent   (8) _____ Other (Specify _____)
   (3) _____ Both Parents   (9) _____ Unknown
   (4) _____ Relatives

6) Please specify Current Charge(s) for which the victim was confined at time of suicide and whether victim was being Detained or had been Committed on those charge(s).

Charge(s)	Detained	Committed
_____	(1) _____	(1) _____
_____	(2) _____	(2) _____
_____	(3) _____	(3) _____

7) Did the victim have a record of Prior Arrests?

      (1) _____ Yes   (2) _____ No

8) If the victim had a prior arrest record, specify the Prior Charges.

      Prior Charge(s)   Date

    _____   _____
    _____   _____
    _____   _____

9) What was the total Length of Confinement that the victim had been in your facility prior to his/her death? If less than two days, indicate in hours.)

    _____ Hours   _____ Days   _____ Months   _____ Years

10) Did the victim have a history of Substance Abuse either in the facility and/or in the community?

    (1) _____ Yes   (2) _____ No   (9) _____ Unknown

11) If the victim had a history of substance abuse, briefly Describe Substance Abuse. _____

12) Did the victim have a history of Medical Problems either in the facility and/or in the community?

    (1) _____ Yes   (2) _____ No   (9) _____ Unknown

13) If the victim had a history of medical problems, briefly Describe Medical Problems. _____

14) Did the victim have a history of Emotional Abuse either in the facility and/or in the community?

    (1) _____ Yes   (2) _____ No   (9) _____ Unknown

15) If the victim had a history of emotional abuse, briefly Describe Emotional Abuse. _____

16) Did the victim have a history of Physical Abuse either in the facility and/or in the community?

    (1) _____ Yes   (2) _____ No   (9) _____ Unknown

17) If the victim had a history of physical abuse, briefly Describe Physical Abuse. _____

18) Did the victim have a history of Sexual Abuse either in the facility and/or in the community?

       (1) _____ Yes   (2) _____ No   (9) _____ Unknown

19) If the victim had a history of sexual abuse, briefly Describe Sexual Abuse. _____
_____
_____
_____

20) Did the victim have a history of mental Illness either in the facility and/or in the community?

       (1) _____ Yes   (2) _____ No   (9) _____ Unknown

21) If the victim had a history of mental illness, briefly Describe mental Illness. _____
_____
_____
_____

22) Did the victim have a history of taking Psychotropic Medication either in the facility and/or in the community?

       (1) _____ Yes   (2) _____ No   (9) _____ Unknown

23) If the victim had a history of taking psychotropic medication, briefly Describe Psychotropic Medication (e.g., date, type, does, and frequency). _____
_____
_____
_____

24) Did the victim have a history of Suicidal behavior either in the facility and/or in the community?

       (1) _____ Yes   (2) _____ No   (9) _____ Unknown

25) If the victim had a history of suicidal behavior, briefly Describe Suicidal behavior. _____
_____
_____
_____

26) Did the victim have a history of Room Confinement (e.g., isolation, segregation, time-out, quiet room, etc., see definitions on page 7) while in the facility?

       (1) _____ Yes   (2) _____ No   (9) _____ Unknown

27) If the victim had a history of room confinement, briefly Describe Types and Circumstances of Room Confinement. ___
_____
_____
_____

PART B: SUICIDE INCIDENT CHARACTERISTICS

28) What was the Date and Time of the victim's suicide?

Date: ___/___/199__   Time (found): _____ a m. _____ p m.

29) What was the Method of suicide and the Instrument used?

<table>
<tr><td>Method</td><td colspan="2">Instrument</td></tr>
<tr><td>(1) _____ Hanging (from _____)</td><td>(01) _____ Shoelace</td><td>(08) _____ Knife</td></tr>
<tr><td>(2) _____ Overdose</td><td>(02) _____ Belt</td><td>(09) _____ Glass</td></tr>
<tr><td>(3) _____ Cutting</td><td>(03) _____ Other Clothing</td><td>(10) _____ Drugs</td></tr>
<tr><td>(4) _____ Shooting</td><td>(04) _____ Bedding</td><td>Specify: _____</td></tr>
<tr><td>(5) _____ Jumping</td><td>(05) _____ Towel</td><td></td></tr>
<tr><td>(6) _____ Ingestion of Foreign Object(s)</td><td>(06) _____ Razor</td><td></td></tr>
<tr><td>(8) _____ Other</td><td>(07) _____ Other (Specify _____)</td><td></td></tr>
</table>

30) At the time of the suicide, was the victim Under the Influence of:

(1) _____ Drugs   (4) _____ Neither Drugs or Alcohol
(2) _____ Alcohol (3) _____ Drugs and Alcohol

31) At the time of the suicide, was the victim assigned to a Single or Multiple Occupancy room?

(1) _____ Single   (2) _____ Multiple

32) What was the Time Span between the suicide and finding the victim?

(1) _____ Less Than 15 Minutes   (4) _____ Between 1 and 3 Hours
(2) _____ Between 15 and 30 Minutes   (5) _____ Greater Than 3 Hours
(3) _____ Between 30 and 60 Minutes

33) Was the victim under any type of Room Confinement (e.g., isolation, segregation, time-out, quiet room, etc.) at the time of the suicide?

(1) _____ Yes   (2) _____ No

34) If the victim was under room confinement at the time of suicide, briefly Describe Type and Circumstances of Room confinement.

_____
_____
_____
_____
_____
_____

35) Was the victim under Suicide Watch (see definitions on page 7) at the time of the suicide?

(1) _____ Yes   (2) _____ No

36) If the victim was under suicide watch at the time of the suicide, what was the Frequency of Staff Observation (excluding any closed circuit television monitoring)?

(1) _____ Continuous   (5) _____ Every 30 Minutes
(2) _____ Every 5 Minutes   (6) _____ Every 60 Minutes
(3) _____ Every 10 Minutes   (8) _____ Other (Specify _____)
(4) _____ Every 15 Minutes

37) Was the victim ever Assessed by a Qualified Mental Health Professional (see definitions on page 7) prior to the suicide?

(1) _____ Yes   (2) _____ No

38) If the victim was assessed, when was the Last Contact by a Qualified Mental Health Professional prior to the suicide? (If less than two days, indicate in hours.)

_____ Hours   _____ Days   _____ Months   _____ Years

39) Was a Mortality Review (see definitions on page 7) conducted following the suicide?

(1) _____ Yes   (2) _____ No

40) If a mortality review was conducted, did the process offer any Possible Precipitating Factors (i.e., circumstances which may have caused the victim to commit suicide)? If yes, describe: _____

41) If a mortality review was conducted, did the process offer any Recommendations to Prevent Future Suicides? If yes, describe: _____

PART C: FACILITY CHARACTERISTICS

42) The Facility (see definitions on page 7) is best described as a:

_____ DETENTION CENTER
_____ TRAINING SCHOOL/SECURE FACILITY
_____ RECEPTION/DIAGNOSTIC CENTER
_____ RANCH, CAMP or FARM
_____ OTHER (Explain): _____

43) The facility is Administered by:

(1) _____ State   (4) _____ Private Organization
(2) _____ County   (8) _____ Other (Specify _____)
(3) _____ Municipality

44) At the time of the suicide, what was the rated Capacity and Population of the facility?

(1) _____ Capacity (2) _____ Population

45) At the time of the suicide, did the facility have a Written Suicide Prevention Policy?

(1) _____ Yes   (2) _____ No

46) At the time of the suicide, did the facility have an Intake Screening process to Identify suicide Risk?

(1) _____ Yes   (2) _____ No

47) At the time of the suicide, had *all* direct-care facility staff received Suicide Prevention Training?

(1) _____ Yes   (2) _____ No

48) If all direct-care facility staff had received suicide prevention training, what was the Frequency and Duration of the Suicide Prevention Training at the time of the suicide?

Frequency	Duration
(1) _____ Yearly	(01) _____ Hours (Specify Number)
(6) _____ Other (Specify _____)	(02) _____ Minutes (Specify Number)

49) At the time of the suicide, had all direct-care facility staff received Certification on Cardiopulmonary Resuscitation?

(1) _____ Yes   (2) _____ No

50) At the time of the suicide, did the facility have a Suicide Watch process (excluding any closed circuit television monitoring)?

(1) _____ Yes   (2) _____ No

51) If the facility had a suicide watch process at the time of the suicide, what was the Frequency Level(s) of Staff Observation? (Check all that apply.)

(1) _____ Continuous   (5) _____ Every 30 Minutes
(2) _____ Every 5 Minutes   (6) _____ Every 60 Minutes
(3) _____ Every 10 Minutes   (8) _____ Other (Specify _____)
(4) _____ Every 15 Minutes

52) At the time of the suicide, did the facility have a Housing process by which a suicidal resident would be assigned to a safe and protrusion-free room?

(1) _____ Yes   (2) _____ No

THE FOLLOWING WILL BE USED FOR INTERNAL PURPOSES ONLY:

Completed by (name/title): _____

Name of Facility: _____

Address (street): _____

    City: _____ State: _____ Zip code: _____

Telephone: _____

Date Completed: _____

Would you like to receive a copy of the survey findings?

        (1) _____ Yes   (2) _____ No

....

DEFINITIONS

ROOM CONFINEMENT: Behavioral sanction imposed on youth that restricts movement for varying amounts of time. Includes, but is not limited to, isolation, segregation, time-out, quiet room.

SUICIDE WATCH: The level(s) of staff observation given to youth identified as being at risk of suicide. Excludes closed circuit television or any other non-staff monitoring.

QUALIFIED MENTAL HEALTH PROFESSIONAL: An individual by virtue of their education, credentials, and experience that is permitted by law to evaluate and care for the mental health needs of patients. May include, but is not limited to, a psychiatrist, psychologies, clinical social worker, and psychiatric nurse.

MORTALITY REVIEW: An interdisciplinary committee process that examines the events surrounding the d4eath to determine if the incident was preventable. the review process may include recommendations aimed at reducing the opportunity for future deaths.

DETENTION CENTER/HOME: A short-term facility that provides custody in a physically restricting environment pending adjudication or, following, adjudication, pending disposition, placement, or transfer.

TRAINING SCHOOL/SECURE FACILITY: A long-term facility for adjudicated youth typically under strict physical/staff controls.

RECEPTION/DIAGNOSTIC CENTER: A short-term facility that screens youth committed by courts and assigns them to appropriate facilities.

RANCH, CAMP, or FARM: A long-term residential facility for youth whose behavior does not require the strict confinement of a training school, often allowing them greater contact with the community. Includes "residential treatment facility" and "boot camp."

....

THANK YOU FOR YOUR COOPERATION

Please return this completed questionnaire in the enclosed business reply envelope within 30 days to:

NCIA
40 Lantern Lane
Mansfield, MA 02048
or fax to
508/337-3083

www.ingramcontent.com/pod-product-compliance
Lightning Source LLC
Chambersburg PA
CBHW082303200526
45168CB00017B/2761